The

THE ETERNAL PRIESTHOOD

HENRY EDWARD MANNING,

CARDINAL ARCHBISHOP OF WESTMINSTER.

"*Tu es sacerdos in aeternum.*" — Heb.v.6.

A reprint of the

Eighth Edition

LONDON: BURNS AND OATES, Limited

NEW YORK: CATHOLIC PUBLICATION SOCIETY CO.

Originally Printed: 1884
Copyright: 2014

TO THE PRIESTS OF

THE DIOCESE OF WESTMINSTER,

IN MEMORY OF

MAKY HAPPY YEARS OF UNITED LABOUR

IN THE SEEVICE OF OUR DIVINE MASTER,

AS A PLEDGE ALSO OF

LOVE MORE LASTING THAN LIFE,

IS INSCRIBED.

ORATIO S. GREGORTI MAGNI ANGLORUM APOSTOLI.

Deus qui nos pastores in populo vocare voluisti praesta quaesumus, ut hoc quod humano ore dicimur, in tuis oculis esse valeamus, per Dominum nostrum Jesum Christum, qui vivit et regnat in unitate Spiritus Sancti Deus, per omnia saecula saeculorum. Amen.

(Opp. tom. i. p. 1400.)

CONTENTS.

Forward 7

CHAPTER:

I. The Nature of Priesthood 11

II. The Powers of the Priesthood 21

III. The Three Relations of the Priesthood 32

IV. The Obligations to Sanctity in the Priesthood 42

V. The Instrumental Means of Perfection ...53

VI. The End of the Priest 63

VII. The Priest's Dangers 73

VIII. The Priest's Helps 83

IX. The Pastoral Office a Source of Confidence ..97

X. The Value op a Priest's Time 107

XI. The Priest's Sorrows 117

XII. The Priest under False Accusation 129

XIII. The Priest's Friend 137

XIV. The Priest as Preacher 149

XV. The Priest's Liberty 161

XVI. The Priest's Obedience …..175

XVII. The Priest's Rewards …..186

XVIII. The Priest's House …..200

XIX. The Priest's Life …..216

XX. The Priest's Death …..228

Forward

For the twenty-first century reader, this work by Henry Edward Cardinal Manning might seem a bit foreign, although it was written at the end of the nineteenth century. Even for priests, much of what Cardinal Manning takes for granted regarding the nature of the priesthood may be unknown. Yet the priesthood of Our Lord Jesus Christ remains the same- yesterday, today, and forever.

Why has such a revolution in thought occurred? It is not the purpose of this forward to examine the nature of the change that has occurred within the Church in the understanding of the very nature of what it means to be a priest. Suffice it to say, that since the time of the Second Vatican Council, a spiritual earthquake has taken place throughout the world, so that many truths formerly held as unshakeable, and indeed, unquestionable, have in fact been either denied, or at least put into question.

The laity, and even priests, seem to have lost the Church's understanding of the nature of the priesthood. This sometimes has sprung simply from the fact that the former understanding was never taught in the modern seminaries, and so priests have been formed, or rather, malformed according to a model that makes the priest simply a facilitator in the liturgy, or even a kind of social worker. There has been a fear to boldly proclaim the fact that a priest is unlike other men; that he has been set aside or consecrated as a mediator between God and man; that he is one who on the one hand offers the

Holy Sacrifice of the Mass to God in propitiation of sin, while at the same time, bringing to man the gifts of God for their salvation. The sanctuaries have been invaded by a gaggle of laymen or laywomen, taking over the functions once reserved to either the priest, or to those who have been deputed to stand in the place of those in minor orders. The distinction between priest and layman has been blurred, and this blurring has led to a confusion regarding the very nature of the Catholic priesthood.

    The great merit of this work by Cardinal Manning is that the priest is reminded of the great grace accorded to him by Almighty God- that he might share in the very priesthood of Jesus Christ Himself, a priest according to the order of Melchisedech. The ordination to the priesthood is not simply a kind of delegation wherein one of the baptised may now preside at the table of the Eucharist, but a consecration that sets the priest utterly apart. He has been taken up into the realm of the Divine, and is forever, for good or ill, marked with the sacred character that gives him the power both over the Sacred Body of Christ in the Blessed Sacrament, and over his Mystical Body which is the Holy Church. Such a dignity, exceeding all earthly dignities, requires of the priest to be the "man of God"- given over to God and to the continuation of the work of the Redemption as an instrument of Jesus Christ the High Priest. Cardinal Manning reminds every priest of his high calling and the supernatural nature and end of the priesthood.

    A priest cannot be a man like other men simply speaking. He is a priest of God, a priest of

Jesus Christ, who must therefore live a divine and supernatural life, if he is to be faithful to his vocation. Cardinal Manning's book has the merit of being clear on this point, both doctrinally and practically. Such a book cannot help but find a response in the heart of any priest of God who seeks to be faithful to the perennial vocation to holiness, as well as to Christ's desire that he be conformed to the model of His own priesthood. May this book be the means that Christ our Lord uses to instruct or even to remind priests of who they are, and of what Christ wishes them to be.

      Fr. Dominic Mary of the Pillar, OP
      Feast of St. Bernard of Clairvaux 2014

THE ETERNAL PRIESTHOOD.

CHAPTER I.

THE NATURE OF PRIESTHOOD.

"Forasmuch as no act can be more excellent than the consecration of the Body of Christ, there can be no order after (i.e. higher than) the priesthood.[1] "No act is greater than the consecration of the Body of Christ."[2] "The Bishop and the priest are equal in respect to the consecration of the Holy Eucharist." S. John Chrysostom founds the sanctity of the priesthood, which, in Bishop and priest, is all one, upon the twofold jurisdiction over the natural and the mystical Body of Christ — that is, upon the power of consecration and upon the power of absolution.[3]

It is of divine faith that our Lord ordained the Apostles to be priests when by the words *hoc facite in mcam commemorationem,* He thereby conferred on them the power of sacrifice.[4] It is also of divine faith that when, three days later, He breathed on them, saying, "Receive ye the Holy Ghost," He gave them the power of absolution.[5] In these two powers the priesthood was complete. The pastoral authority

---

[1] Albertus M. in lib. iv. Sent. dist. xxiv. art. 30.
[2] S. Thom. *Summa Theol.* lib. iii. in Suppl. q. 40, a. 4, 5.
[3] De Sacerdotio lib. iii. § 4, 5.
[4] Conc. Trid. sess. xx. c. ix. canon 2.
[5] Ibid. sess. xiv. c. iii. canon 3.

and the world-wide commission of the Apostles were not yet given. They had received the twofold jurisdiction over His natural body and over the mystical body, together with the power of bestowing the same by ordination upon others, for their priesthood was the "*sacerdotium Christi ad Ecclesiam regendam a Spiritui Sancto positum.*"

In conferring the same afterwards, they bestowed this sacerdotal office upon some in all its fulness — that is, with the power of bestowing it upon others; and on some, with the limitation that the priest ordained could not confer upon others the sacerdotal jurisdiction which he had received. Excepting this alone, the priesthood in the Bishop and the priesthood in the priest are one and the same, and yet the Episcopate, by the divine power of ordination, is greater than the priesthood. But this difference is divine and incommunicable. S. Jerome says: *Quid enim facit, excepta ordinatione Episcopus quod presbyter non faciat.*[6]

It is of faith that the Episcopate is the state of perfection instituted by Jesus Christ. It is certain also that the priesthood is included in that state. Whatsoever is true of the priesthood in itself is true both of Bishop and of priest. And in this we see why at first the names were for a while common and interchanged. The injunctions of Christian perfection given by S. Paul to Timothy and to Titus were given to Bishop and to presbyter or priest alike.[7] And the whole book of S. John Chrysostom, *De Sacerdotio*, expressly applies equally to both.

---

[6] S. Hieron. Epist. ci. ad Evangelum, tom. iv. p. 803.
[7] Theodoret in Ep. ad Phil. i. 1.

S. Thomas says that priests partake of the priesthood of our Divine Lord, and that they are configured or conformed to Him. Let us therefore weigh the words priesthood, participation, and configuration, as here used.

1. What, then, is the priesthood of the Incarnate Son?[8] It is the office He assumed for the redemption of the world by the oblation of Himself in the vestment of our manhood. He is Altar, Victim, and Priest, by an eternal consecration of Himself. This is the priesthood for ever after the order of Melchisedech, who was "without beginning of days or end of life"[9] — a type of the eternal priesthood of the Son of God, the only King of Peace.

2. By participation, S. Thomas means that the priesthood of Jesus Christ being the one, only, perpetual, and universal priesthood, all priests consecrated under the New Law are made one with Him, and share in His own priesthood.[10] There are not two priesthoods, as there are not two sacrifices for sin. But one sacrifice has for ever redeemed the world, and is offered continually in heaven and on earth: in heaven by the only Priest, before the

---

[8] "Proprie officium sacerdotis est esse mediatorem inter Deum et populum, inquantum scilicet divina populo tradit." — Summa S. Thoma, P. iii. q. xxii. a. 1.
"Et ideo ipse Christus, inquantum homo, non solum fait sacerdos, sed etiam hostia perfecta, simul existens hostia pro peccato, et hostia pacifica, et holocaustum." — Ibid. a. 2.

[9] Heb. vii. 3.

[10] P. iii. q. lxiii. 6, and q. xxii. 5, 6.

Eternal Altar; on earth by the multitude and succession of priests who are one with Him as partakers of His priesthood; not as representatives only, but in reality; as also the sacrifice they offer is not a representation only, but His true, real, and substantial Body and Blood offered by their hands.

This is the argument of the Epistle to the Hebrews. The priesthood of the Old Law was a shadow; the priesthood of the New Law is the substance. It is fulfilled in the one Priest and the one Sacrifice which are perpetuated by the priesthood, on earth united with Him.

But this participation has another and more personal meaning. The oblation of our Lord for us binds us to offer ourselves wholly to Him. *Christus …victima sacerdotii sui, et sacerdos suae victimae fuit… Ipsi sunt hostiae sacerdotes*[11] S. Ambrose, speaking of the sacrifice of Abel, says: *Hoc est sacrificium primitivum, quando unus quisque se offert hostiam, et a se incipit ut postea munus suum possit offerre.*[12] Priests offer the true Lamb and "the Blood which speaketh better things than that of Abel."[13] Every priest, morning by morning, offers to the Father the eternal oblation of Jesus Christ; but in that action he ought to offer also himself. When he says. *Hoc est corpus meum*, he ought to offer his own body; when he says. *Hic est calix sanguinis mei*, he ought to offer his own blood; that is, he ought to offer himself as an oblation to his Divine Master, in body, soul, and spirit, with all his faculties, powers, and affections, in life and unto

---

[11] S. Paulinus, Ep. xi. § 8, ad Severum.
[12] De Abel. lib. ii. c. vi. tom, i, p. 215.
[13] Heb, xii. 24.

death. S. Paul writes to the Philippians, "If I be made a victim upon the sacrifice and service of your faith, I rejoice and congratulate with you all."[14] This it may be he also said of the martyrdom which was before him; but it was spoken out of the consciousness that he had long and daily offered himself to his Divine Master, as a partaker of His sufferings for the sake of the elect.[15] The same words might have been written by S. John, who always had a martyr's will, though he died in the way of nature; the same, too, is implied in every Mass, by every priest who offers himself in the Holy Sacrifice of the Altar. The participation of the priest in the priesthood of Christ requires also a share in the law of self-oblation, of which the prophet writes: *Oblatus est quia ipse voluit*; and S. Paul, who says of our Lord that He, "by the Holy Ghost, offered Himself unspotted unto God."[16] And, as S. John says, "in this we have known the charity of God, because He hath laid down His life for us, and we ought to lay down our lives for the brethren."[17] "The offering of the Body and Blood of Christ requires of the priest a spirit of self-sacrifice and of self-oblation without reserve. The obligation of charity, which binds all Christians, when the need may arise, to lay down their lives for the brethren, and pastors to give their life for the sheep, is in an especial way laid upon every priest in the self-oblation of the Holy Mass, which is the Sacrifice of Jesus Christ.

---

[14] Phil. ii. 17.
[15] 2 S. Tim. iv. 6,7,8
[16] Heb. ix. 14.
[17] 1 S. John iii. 16.

3. Lastly, the word configuration expresses the conformity of the priest to the great High Priest. S. Paul says that the Son is *figura substantiae ejus* — that is, the figure or express image of the substance of the Father. The Greek text reads, χαραχτηρ τησ υποστασωσ υποστασεωσ αυτου , the character of His substance.[18] The priest, then, is the *figura Christi*, the express image of Christ, the χαραχτηρ or character of Christ, because upon him is impressed the image of His priesthood, and a share in it is given to him. He is, as S. Paul says, *configuratus morti ejus*[19] — configured to His death. In every Mass we set forth "the death of the Lord until He come."[20] And we make oblation of ourselves in conformity to His oblation to the Father. Albertus Magnus and S. Thomas have said truly that no greater power or dignity, than the power and dignity of consecrating the Body of Christ, was ever bestowed on man; and no greater sanctity or perfection can be conceived than the sanctity and perfection required for so divine an action in the priest.

S. Thomas tells us that ordination impresses a character, and that the character is a spiritual and indelible sign or seal, by which the soul is marked for the exercise of the acts of divine worship, and for the teaching of the same to others.[21] The priesthood

---

[18] Heb. i, 3.

[19] Phil. iii. 10.

[20] 1 Cor. xi. 26

[21] "Per omnia Sacramenta fit homo particeps sacerdotii Christi, utpote percipiens aliquem effectum ejus; non tamen per omnia Sacrameuta aliquis deputalur ad agendum aliquid, vel recipiendum quod pertineat ad cultum sacerdotii Christi; quod quidem exigitur ad hoc quod Sacramentum characterem

of Christ is the source of all divine worship.[22] All the faithful are conformed to Christ by the character impressed upon them in Baptism and Confirmation: and priests also in Ordination.[23] But in Christ Himself there was no character, because He is the exemplar and type of all characters; for Christ is the Character or Figure of the Father, and all divine perfection is in Him, of which the character in us is a partial conformity.[24] The character we receive is impressed, not on the essence, but on the powers of the soul — that is, on the intellectual or the affective powers — and is either passive or active.[25] The character of Baptism is a passive power for the reception of all other Sacraments, and for

---

imprimat." — Summa S. Thomas, P. iii. q. lxiii. a. 6.

"Character proprie est signaculum quoddam quo aliquid insignitur, ut ordinatum in aliquem finen." Ibid. a. 3.
"Character ordinatur ad ea quae sunt divini cultus." Ibid. a. 4.

[22] "Totus autem ritus Christianae religionis derivatur a sacerdotio Christi." Ibid. a.3.

[23] Pertinet autem aliquod Sacramentum ad divinum cultum tripliciter: uno modo per modum ipsius actionis; alio modo per modum agentis; tertio modo per modum recipieutis… Sed ad agens in Sacramentis pertinet Sacramentum ordinis… Sed ad recipientes pertinet Sacramentum baptismi… Ad idem etiam ordinatur quoddammodo confirmatio… Et ideo per haec tria Sacramenta character imprimitur, scilicet per baptismum, confirmationem, et ordinem," Ibid. a. 6.

[24] "Et propter hoc etiam Christo non conpetit habere characterem; sed potestas sacerdotii ejus comparatur ad characterem sicut id quod est plenum, et perfectum ad aliquam sui participationem." Ibid. a. 5.

[25] "Character est quoddam signaculum quo anima insignitur ad suscipiendum, vel aliis tradendum ea quae sunt divini cultus. Divinus autem cultus in quibusdam actibus consistit. Ad actus autem proprie ordinantur potentiae animae, sicut essentia ordinatur ad esse. Et ideo character non est sicut in subjecto in essentia animae, sed in ejus potentia." Ibid. a. 4.

conformity as sons to the Son of God. The character of Confirmation is an active power for the public witness of the faith, and for the life of action and of patience as good soldiers of Christ. The character of Ordination is an active power for the exercise and ministry of divine worship. [26] The sacerdotal character, therefore, is a participation of the priesthood of Christ and the closest configuration to Him in His office of mediator. Finally, this character is the cause and source of sacramental grace, proper to each of the three Sacraments which impress it, and commensurate to their ends and obligations.

The word "character" means the precise outline of an engraving, as on a seal, and the impression of it signifies that a mark or reproduction of the same outline, as by a signet, is left upon the soul. This is clearly a metaphor, as also is the sealing of the hundred and forty-four thousand before the four winds shall blow upon the earth. S. Thomas, in saying that the character is impressed, not on the essence of the soul, but upon its powers, means on the intellect by way of light, and on the affections by way of love.

It signifies therefore a work of the Holy Ghost the Illuminator and Sanctifier upon the soul. But it signifies not only the universal and uniform

---

[26] "Divinus autem cultus consistit vel in recipiendo aliqua divina vel in tradendo aliis. Ad utrumque autem horum requiritur quaedam potentia: nam ad tradendum aliquid aliis requiritur quaedam potentia activa; ad accipiendum autem requiritur potentia passiva. Et ideo character importat quamdam potentiam spiritualem ordinatam ad ea quae sunt divini cultus." Ibid. a. 3, and q. lxxii. a. 5.

work of the Holy Ghost, as in Baptism and Confirmation; but a special and singular work wrought upon the soul of those only who by Ordination share in the priesthood of Jesus Christ. The three Sacraments which impress a character create and constitute each severally a special relation of the soul to God: Baptism that of sons, Confirmation that of soldiers, Orders that of priests; and these three spiritual relations once constituted are eternal, and therefore indelible. Whether in the light of glory or in the outer darkness, we shall be sons, soldiers, and priests, accepted or cast out eternally. And to these three relations a special and commensurate grace of the Holy Ghost is attached. Therefore, S. Thomas says that the character is the formal cause or source of sacramental grace.[27] The character of son has in it all grace needed for the life of a son of God; the character of confirmation all grace needed for the warfare of the soldiers of Jesus Christ, even to confessorship and martyrdom; the character of priesthood has in it all graces of light, strength, and sanctity needed for the sacerdotal life in all its manifold duties, trials, and dangers. It was of this S. Paul reminded S. Timothy when he said, "Neglect not the grace that is in thee, which was given thee by prophecy, with imposition of the hands of the priesthood."[28]

Such is the priesthood of the Son of God, the consecration and oblation of Himself: and such is its communication to His priests by participation in His office, by configuration to Himself, and by

---

[27] P. iii. lxix, 10.
[28] 1 S. Tim. iv. 14.

the impression of the sacerdotal character upon the powers of the soul.

CHAPTER II.

THE POWERS OF THE PRIESTHOOD.

S. John Chrysostom sums up the powers of a priest in these two; namely, the consecration of the Sacrament of the Altar, and the absolution of sin, or, as we say in theological terms, in the jurisdiction over the natural and over the mystical Body of Christ. The word jurisdiction has here a special significance. It means usually the authority by which a priest rules the flock committed to him with the judicial power of binding and loosing the bond of sin. How, then, can there be jurisdiction over the Blessed Sacrament? Jurisdiction signifies the whole sacerdotal authority given in ordination, but its exercise is suspended until the priest shall have received license to use the powers of his priesthood. This jurisdiction comes to him from his Bishop, and to his Bishop from the Vicar of Jesus Christ, in whom alone resides the plenitude of jurisdiction over the universal Church. The first and highest act of that jurisdiction is to consecrate and to offer the Holy Sacrifice of the Altar. Hence arises the expression of jurisdiction *in corpus verum*, which words, nevertheless, have also many deep meanings.

1. First, they set before us the humility of our Divine Master. The Incarnation was a descent which had many degrees. He emptied Himself by veiling His glory; He took the form of a servant; He was made man; He humbled Himself; and that to death; and to die in ignominy. Here are six degrees of humiliation. And as if these were not enough, He perpetuates His humility in the Blessed Sacrament,

and places Himself in the hands of His creatures, and is bid,[29] morning by morning, by their word to be present upon the altar; and is by them lifted up, and carried to and fro, and, in the end, He is received by the worthy and by the unworthy. In this divine manner He subjects Himself to the jurisdiction of His priests now, as in the days of His earthly life He was subject to the law, and to those who bore authority, even to Caiaphas and to Pilate. Humility is the root of all obedience; and patience is obedience made perfect. The oblation of Himself is obedience continued for ever as the law and motive of His priests.

2. Next, this power of jurisdiction implies the divine stewardship which is intrusted to the priest. The Church applies to S. Joseph, the foster-father of the Divine Infant, the words of the Holy Ghost: "He that keepeth the fig-tree shall eat the fruit thereof, and he that is the keeper of his master shall be glorified." [30] The guardianship of the Blessed Sacrament is in the priest. The key of the tabernacle is committed to his trust. It may be said of him, as of his Master, that "he openeth and no man shutteth, he shutteth and no man openeth."[31] The priest is, in the truest sense of the word, the guardian of his Lord; and no greater glory can be laid upon him; no relation more intimate, close, and ceaseless can be conceived.

And this stewardship is also a power to dispense and to distribute the bread of life. The

---

[29] "Obediente Domino voci hominis" (Josue x. 14).

[30] Prov. xxvii. 18.

[31] Apoc. iii. 7.

disciples gave it to the five thousand in the wilderness. "They were ministers of Christ, and dispensers of the mysteries of God."[32] And in this they were shadows of the divine reality of Holy Communion, of which we are stewards.

3. Thirdly, this jurisdiction shows the divine power inherent in the priesthood. The words we speak are not ours, but His; not human, but divine. "This is My Body" has no equal, except "Let the light be." These words created the light. The other words do not create; but they constitute, or bring upon the altar, the presence of the Incarnate Word. They elevate the bread and the wine from the natural to the supernatural order. This is a power, not creative, but of omnipotence. The bread and the wine are no longer subject to the conditions or laws of nature as to their substance, but only as to their sensible phenomena. A divine change passes upon them: and yet not a natural change; for they pass away as to their substance, and yet abide as to their sensible effects. There is no such change in the order of nature; for there the whole natural substance and accidents either abide, or go together. Here the phenomena or sensible species and effects abide, as if they were in the natural order. The substance passes away in the supernatural order of the new creation. The words, "Let the light be," had their effect in the first creation of nature. The words, "This is My Body," have their effect on the first creation and in the second; in both the old creation and the new. They stand next in order to the words, "The Holy Ghost shall come upon thee, and the power of the Highest shall overshadow thee;

---

[32] 1 Cor. iv. 1.

therefore that Holy (One) which shall be born of thee shall be called the Son of God."[33] For this cause the action of consecration and the action of the Incarnation are related to each other. Next to the Incarnation there is no action so transcendent, so purely divine, as the consecration and the Holy Sacrifice. It is the continuity of the Incarnation and Oblation of the Incarnate Son. The voice that speaks the words is human; the words and the effects are of the almighty power of God.

4. Fourthly, this jurisdiction expresses the intimate closeness of the relation between the priest and the Son of God. It would seem that, after the participation of His priesthood, the impression of His character, and the configuration of the priest to his Divine Master, there is no relation left to be conceived. And yet there are two still to be spoken of. First, there is the continual daily fellowship of the disciple with his Master, and the servant with his Lord. He is servant, friend, companion. As Peter, James, and John were of all the disciples nearest to our Saviour upon earth, so are His priests among the faithful now. All the daylong they are near to Him; all their life is related to Him. From Him they go out in the morning, and to Him they return at night.

Next, there is the relation of a true, substantial, and living contact in the Holy Mass as real as when S. John lay on His bosom at supper, or as when He washed S. Peter's feet. When we hold the Blessed Sacrament in our hands we are in contact with God, with God Incarnate, with the Creator,

---

[33] S. Luke i. 35.

Redeemer, and Sanctifier. More real than the earth under our feet, which will pass away, is the presence of the Incarnate Word, which will never pass away. We are in contact with His substance. "He who is joined to the Lord is one spirit." But we are also united to the substance of His Body; and we are members of it by a real and substantial participation. S. Paul says that we are "members of His Body, of His flesh, and of His bone,"[34] and he bids us to "bear God in our body."[35] This contact and union is eternal life. If, as we hold the Blessed Sacrament in our hands, our eyes were opened like the eyes of Cleophas at Emmaus, we should know that beyond this sacramental and substantial contact there is nothing more intimate, except union with Him in the light of glory.

Such, then, are the reasons which have illuminated the teachers of the Church to know that there can be conceived no office higher, and no power greater, than the office and power of a priest. In the order of divine actions it places the priest, in respect to the power of consecration, next to the Blessed Virgin, the living tabernacle of the Incarnate Word; and, in respect to the guardianship of the Blessed Sacrament, next to S. Joseph, the foster-father and guardian of the Son of God. What more can be bestowed upon the priest? What obligation to perfection can exceed the obligation of such a power, of such an office, and of such a living contact with the Word made flesh? S. John Chrysostom says the hand that consecrates ought to be purer than the solar light; and if the hand of the

---

[34] Ephes. V. 30.
[35] 1 Cor. vi. 20.

priest, what should be his eyes which gaze upon the Divine Presence, veiled but hardly hidden, and the lips which say, "This is My Body," and the ears that hear our own familiar voice uttering these words of the new creation of God? But if such should be the sanctity of the body, what should be the purity of the soul of the priest: in his intellect, with all its powers, faculties, memory, imagination; in his heart, with all its affections and desires; in his conscience, with all its discernment and sovereign commands; and in his will, with all its inflexible resolves and steadfast reign over his whole outward and inward life?

Surely, then, the priesthood is by its own nature, requirements, and obligations an essential rule, and the highest state of perfection divinely instituted by our Lord Himself.

But this is not all. The priest has also jurisdiction over the mystical Body of Christ — that is, over the souls of those who are born again of water and the Holy Ghost. S. Paul says, "We are the good odour of Christ unto God in them that are saved and in them that perish. To the one, indeed, the odour of death unto death; but to the others, the odour of life unto life. And for these things who is so sufficient?"[36] That is, who shall not fear? What can be more formidable than to stand between the living and the dead, charged with the priestly office, to give account for the souls committed to our trust? The Fathers call it an office which angels fear to bear. To be a king over a people, or a leader over an army in which the earthly life of men is at stake,

---

[36] 2 Cor. ii. 15, 16.

is formidable. How much more is a superiority the effects of which are eternal? What sanctity, what charity, what humility, what patience, what wisdom, what firmness, what equity, are "sufficient for these things"? If the relation in which a priest stands to His Divine Lord in the Holy Mass demands spiritual perfection, certainly the relation of teacher, guide, and judge of men demands the same. The priest is set *exercere perfectionem* — that is, to manifest perfection in himself, and to form the souls of men to the same law and likeness. He must needs then be perfect first himself.

The titles by which this relation is illustrated are many, and show how manifold are its obligations. Even under the Old Law the typical priests were described as fishermen,[37] and hunters,[38] and shepherds.[39] Under the New they are called fishers of men,[40] and shepherds[41] of the flock. But they are more than this.

They are stewards set over the household to give to every man meat in due season — that is, to guide and govern the household of God.

They are ambassadors[42] from God, having, therefore, commission to treat and to conclude in His name. They have the credentials of a divine embassy, with express conditions on which to call

---

[37] Jerem. xvi. 16.
[38] Ibid.
[39] Ezech. xxxiv. 23.
[40] S. Mark i. 17.
[41] 1 S. Peter v. 2, 4.
[42] 2 Cor. v. 20.

upon men to reconcile themselves with Him; and with a discretion to judge and to decide who do and who do not come within the terms and conditions of their commission.

They are fellow-workers[43] with God in the field of the world and in the vineyard of the Church. They are ploughers, [44] and sowers [45] and reapers.[46] The priesthood has the office of breaking up the fallow ground of the nations, and of destroying the roots of unbelief[47] that hinder the plough. "I have made thee as a new thrashing wain, with teeth like a saw: thou shalt thrash the mountains and break them in pieces, and shalt make the hills as chaff. Thou shalt fan them, and the wind shall carry them away.[48] They are sowers who cast the seed of the Word upon all lands and beside all waters. [49] They are reapers who go weeping in the midst of a barren and dying world, who shall one day come with joy, bringing their sheaves with them. [50] But these titles, though expressive, are ideal and pictorial. There are others more homely and lying closer to our life and needs.

Priests are also fellow-builders with God in edifying the Church, and rearing the temple of the Holy Ghost upon the one only foundation which

---

[43] 1 Cor. iii. 9.
[44] Ibid. ix. 10.
[45] S. Mark iv. 14.
[46] S. John iv. 38.
[47] Heb. xii. 15.
[48] Isaias xli. 15,16.
[49] Ibid, xxxii. 20
[50] Ps. cxxv. 5-7.

Christ, the Master-builder, has laid. They are fathers of all who are born again by water and the Holy Ghost: but in a special sense, and with a more intimate and an eternal relation, they are fathers of those whom they have baptised. S. Paul says to the Corinthians, "If you have ten thousand instructors in Christ, yet not many fathers, for in Christ Jesus by the Gospel I have regenerated you."[51] This title is the most simple and intelligible to all, old and young, learned and unlettered. The relation of father and child is universal in the order of nature, and it becomes a spiritual instinct in the order of grace. The title of father is the first, the chief, the highest, the most potent, the most persuasive, the most honourable of all the titles of a priest. He may receive from the world and from its fountains of honour many names, from the schools of learning many degrees, from the ecclesiastical law many dignities; but none has so deep and so high a sense as father, and none but the spiritual fatherhood will pass into eternity. The world has overlaid the title of father with its own profuse adulation, and priests have consented to their deprival in accepting the world's addresses. With the title, the consciousness of paternal or filial relation has been first obscured, then forgotten, and in the end lost. The closest bond of mutual confidence and charity between the priesthood and the faithful has been thereby relaxed, and a distance and diffidence has often grown up instead.

Priests are also judges of men. The Jews forbade any man who was not a father to become a judge; for justice must be tempered with

---

[51] 1 Cor. iv. 15.

compassion. But for the spiritual judge more than natural compassion is needed. The spiritual judge needs the charity of God, of whom all paternity or fatherhood in heaven and earth is named. A judge must needs be just, and justice includes mercy. S. Gregory the Great, in explaining the celestial hierarchy, says that the "thrones" are the just, in whom God dwells and reigns, as in the seat of His sovereignty. Our Divine Master said, "Ye that have followed Me, when the Son of Man shall sit on the throne of His glory, ye also shall sit on twelve thrones, judging the twelve tribes of Israel."[52] This was spoken to the Apostles and to the Episcopate, which, in their stead, now succeeds to the spiritual judgment of the world. Each Bishop in his throne, surrounded by his priests, judicially binding or loosing the souls of men by the power of the keys, is the judge of arbitration to avert the judgment of the last day.

Lastly, they are physicians. The priests of the Old Law were taught to discern between leprosy and leprosy, as the priests of the New Law are taught to discern between sin and sin. And for this office two things above all are necessary — science and charity; the science of God, the science of the Saints, the science of self-knowledge; and charity, which, though it will not break the bruised reed, or quench the smoking flax, will never be silent when there is a sickness unto death, or when venial sin may pass into mortal, and the disease of the soul turn to death, S. Paul might well ask, "for these things who is sufficient?" To stand in such close relation to the Word made flesh; to be set over the

---

[52] S. Matt. xix. 28.

souls for whom He shed His Precious Blood; to be charged with their salvation, so that if we be unfaithful their blood will be required at our hands: all this surely demands in the priest a personal sanctity commensurate with the work of guiding souls from sin to penance, and from penance to perfection. How shall they guide who have never trodden the path themselves? Some theologians tell us that a man may exercise perfection— that is, teach others to be perfect who is not perfect himself. The imperfections even of the perfect are many, as the best priest knows better than any man. Nevertheless, to exercise perfection on others requires that the priest should be in the state of perfection, though it be only within the border-line. But no priest can be content with so ungenerous a heart. S. Paul was not so minded when he said, "I do not count myself to have apprehended; but one thing I do: forgetting the things that are behind, and stretching forth myself to those that are before, I press towards the mark to the prize of the supreme vocation of God in Christ Jesus."[53]

---

[53] Philip. iii. 13,14.

CHAPTER III.

THE THREE RELATIONS OF THE PRIESTHOOD.

A PRIEST stands in three relations, of which each one binds him to interior spiritual perfection.

1. The first binds him to the great High Priest, of whose priesthood he is partaker. He is our fountain of sanctity; but He is also our law of obligation. To those who drew near to Him in the priesthood of the Old Law God said, *Sancti estote, quia ego sanctus sum*.[54] The uncreated sanctity of God demands sanctity in all who approach Him. At the burning bush in Horeb God commanded Moses to put off the shoes from his feet; for the ground he stood on was holy.[55] An unholy man, if he seeks the priesthood, is seeking eternal death; for "who can dwell with everlasting burnings?"[56] The holiness, the purity, the jealousy, the justice of God, are as the flames of a furnace, in which the pure are still more purified; but the impure are consumed. *For God is a consuming fire*.[57] Only those who are configured to the High Priest of their salvation, and by a true will desire to be perfectly sanctified in body, soul, and spirit, can stand before Him. On them His sanctity has a power of assimilation, which perfects the work which He began in them when He first called them. Isaias, when he saw the Lord of Hosts in His glory,

---

[54] Levit. xi. 44,46.
[55] Exod. iii. 5.
[56] Isaias xxxiii. 14.
[57] Heb. xii. 29.

was conscious only of his own impurity before Him. But one of the seraphim flew with a live coal from the altar and touched his lips; and his sin was cleansed.[58] The nearer the pure approach to God, the more they are purified. Of the accessions of sanctity in the soul of our spotless Mother through her earthly life by union with her Divine Son, both before and after His ascension, we will not speak; for she was singular in all things, being without sin and sanctified above the seraphim. But we may meditate on the sanctity of S. John and of S. Peter, after their call to follow our Divine Redeemer. The conscious unfitness of S. Peter made him cry out, "Depart from me; for I am a sinful man, O Lord."[59] The miracle of the fishes opened his eyes to the power of Jesus; but it was His sanctity that made him fear to be in His presence. The three years in which the Apostles followed our Lord were their preparation for the priesthood. They had many imperfections, which, as time wore on, were consumed in the sanctity of their Master's presence. They breathed an atmosphere of purity and of perfection. Slow of heart to believe, tardy to understand, hasty in speech, earthly in thought, seeking to be first, and contending with each other which should be the greatest: nevertheless the majesty of their Lord subdued them, and His love reigned over them; and day by day their old minds died in them, and the mind of Jesus Christ grew in them, until it governed them altogether. The work of their purification was always advancing; for the Divine Presence was the refining fire purifying the sons of Levi, and refining them as gold and as silver,

---

[58] Isaias vi. 6,7.
[59] S. Luke v. 8.

that they might offer sacrifices to the Lord in justice.[60] But one of them was a devil — not from childhood, it may be, but from the time when an impure soul came into daily contact with divine purity. It grew daily and gradually, and perhaps insensibly, in impurity, by its conscious variance with the sanctity of Jesus. Judas was ordained in mortal sin; and, after his first Communion, Satan entered into him. For three years he had breathed an atmosphere of sanctity without being sanctified. What should have been for his salvation became an occasion of falling; and the life of the world was turned by him into death.

The relation in which a priest stands to his Divine Master is, in everything except sensible presence, the same as theirs. It is as personal, real, and continuous. We have a Master in heaven.[61] And our loyalty to Him rests on consciousness, not on sight, as in this world our allegiance is paid to a sovereign whom perhaps we have never seen. S. Peter says of this, "Whom having not seen you love: in whom also now, though you see Him not, you believe; and, believing, shall rejoice with joy unspeakable and glorified;"[62] that is, full of the earnest and the foretaste of eternal bliss. It is no mere imagination in our work, early and late, to believe that He is near us, in the ship or on the shore; nor, when we are in the hospital or in the poor man's home, or by the bed of the dying, or walking through the fields, or in the crowded streets, or in the mountains seeking His scattered sheep,

---

[60] Malachias iii. 3.
[61] Ephes. vi. 9,
[62] 1 S. Pet. i. 8.

that He is with us at every step and in every moment. It is no illusion to believe that the words He spoke are spoken still to us, or that every word we speak is spoken in His hearing. When He was on earth, and His disciples round Him, their eyes were not always fixed upon Him, still less were their words and thoughts always directed to Him. They saw all that was around them in the streets, or the fields, or upon the sea, and their thoughts multiplied and, as we say, wandered, and they spoke with one another with the freedom of daily fellowship; but they were always conscious that He was in the midst of them, and that He not only heard their words, but read their thoughts, and answered them before they spoke. In what, except in sense, does our relation differ from theirs? And are not Nazareth and Bethlehem and Jerusalem and Capharnaum and Bethania as real to us as if we had seen them? To those who have faith and knowledge of the Word of God all these things are as real as the daily world around them; and this conscious relation is a wakeful motive and a perpetual discipline in the life of a faithful priest.

2. The second relation is still to our Divine Master, but under a special condition. Jesus is always present in the midst of His pastors unto the consummation of the world — that is, until He shall have gathered out His elect and fulfilled His eternal predestination, and shall wind up the time of grace and the probation of man. As Head of the Church He is in every living member of His mystical Body. But as Head of the Church He is in the glory of the Father, and from the right hand of the Father He never departs till He shall come again to judge the living and the dead. Our relation to Him in heaven

is nevertheless a divine and real dependence. But this is common to all alike. The priesthood has another relation, as we have seen, in the custody of His sacramental Presence. *Mundamini qui fertis vasa Domini*. If they who bore the vessels of the Lord were bound to purity, what is the obligation of the priest, who bears the Lord Himself? A trust is a sign of confidence; to be trusted by God, who knows our hearts, is a pledge of an especial confidence; to be intrusted with the presence of the Incarnate Word is the highest pledge of the most absolute confidence. What a vocation is the call to be a priest. What an integrity and sincerity of heart does it demand. Happy for us if we could think that our Master saw in us what He saw in Nathaniel — a heart in which there is no guile. When He was on earth He did not trust Himself to men, because He knew what was in men.[63] Can it be that He knew what was in us when He committed Himself to us in His sacramental Presence? A token of confidence, even in earthly things, will win the whole heart of a servant to his master. What ought to be the fidelity, loyalty, joy, devotion of our hearts for the custody of His Presence, His Person, and His dignity before men? The Blessed Sacrament consecrates the tabernacle, the altar, the sanctuary, the home of the priest. The bush in Horeb burned; but the priest and all about him are enveloped in the radiance and in the influence of the Blessed Sacrament intrusted to his charge. How can he lose the consciousness of this relation even for a moment? He may not be always in actual advertence to it. Even the disciples, when they picked the ears of wheat, or wondered at the

---

[63] S. John ii. 24,25.

stones of the Temple, or at the withering of the fig-tree, had other thoughts; but they were still conscious of one chief dominant thought which governed all, and continually recalled them to His presence. So it may be — so it ought to be — with us. A priest ought to be in no place where His Master would not go, nor employed in anything which His Master would not do. In the morning the priest spoke the words of almighty power, and for awhile he was in contact with the Incarnate Word. Such a consciousness — for it must not be called a memory as of a thing that is past, but a sustained sense as of a thing that cannot pass away — ought to control his whole life through the whole day. The thought that at night he will return, before he lies down to rest, to the Presence of His Master to give account of the hours and actions of the day ought to be a rule and a restraint upon the senses, the heart, and the lips. The love of a human friend, even in his absence, will govern and guide us: how much more the Presence of a Divine Friend ought to control and elevate our life! S. Gregory says, "O, wonderful condescension of the Divine Goodness! We are not worthy to be servants, and we are called friends. What a dignity for men to be friends of God."[64]

3. There is still a third relation which is of divine ordinance, and, when once constituted, will be found again in eternity: that is to say, the relation between a priest and the souls committed to his charge. This relation may be created in two ways: either by the assignment of a flock by which a priest becomes also a pastor, or by the voluntary choice of those who subject themselves to the guidance of any

---

[64] In S. Joan. xv. 14,15, tom. i. p. 1445.

confessor. In either case, a true relation of eternal consequence at once arises. In speaking of the pastoral relation, the other will, in its proportion, be included, and need not be further treated. That any man should be charged with the salvation of another is a relation of the divine order. By the law of nature, fathers have such a charge of their children while under age and unable to care for themselves. In a few years the father's authority is outgrown, and comes to an end. It is also at all times limited, for over the conscience of children parents have no authority. But in the supernatural order it is the will of God that the fraternal hatred of Cain should be replaced by the fraternal love of pastors. "Am I my brother's keeper?"[65] is the voice of the world. "I am the Good Shepherd"[66] is the voice of our Master laying down for His pastors the law of their life. Under the Old Law, God commanded that a watchman should be set over the people in time of war. If the watchman, seeing the sword coming, gave warning by the trumpet, then, if any man did not look to himself and so should perish his blood was upon his own head, and the watchman was free. But if the watchman should see the sword coming and should give no warning, then the divine sentence was, "I will require his blood at the hands of the watchman."[67] No man could be made answerable for another's life except by the Lord and Giver of life. An office is laid upon the watchman, and a necessity to discharge it, or to answer with his own life for his neglect. He is not answerable for the results of his warning, but only

---

[65] Gen. iv. 9.
[66] S. John x. 14.
[67] Ezech. xxxiii, 2-6.

for his own fidelity. Such also is the pastor's charge. The Lord of the flock puts it into his trust, and he must answer for it with his life. S. Gregory says that a pastor has as many souls of his own as he has sheep in his flock. Who could so charge him but God only, who alone can say, "All souls are mine"?[68] There is, then, a mutual relation of authority and of submission, by divine institution. But what man has authority over another by the law of nature, or unless by direct commission by the supernatural law of grace? Where no authority is, there can be no duty to submit. "Every man shall bear his own burden;"[69] but the burdens of many are laid, by divine command, upon the shepherd of souls. He also is not answerable for the effects of his care, but only for its faithful discharge. When he has given his heart and strength and time, his life, and, if so be, his death, to serve and to save his flock, he may rest in hope. The blood of those that perish will not be required of him. But what zeal, abnegation of self, what generosity and patience, what humility and charity, are needful to bear with the wickedness of the sinful, and the waywardness of the good. The shepherd must go in all things before the flock, or they cannot follow him. He must first have acquired what he is to teach them, and he will teach them less by what he says than by what he is. It is the living word that converts, sustains, and sanctifies the hearts of men. *Summa dicere et ima facere* is a provocation of God and man. The parable of the beam and the mote should be inscribed on the wall in every seminary, and in the conscience of every priest. S. Paul's words are terrible to the priest who

---

[68] Ezech. xviii. 4.

[69] Gal. vi. 5.

is a priest by ordination, but not by sanctity, "Thou makest thy boast of God, and knowest His will, and approvest the more profitable things, being instructed by the law: art confident that thou thyself art a guide of the blind, a light to them that are in darkness, an instructor of the foolish, a teacher of infants, having the form of knowledge and of truth in the law. Thou, therefore, that teachest another, teachest not thyself: thou that preachest that man should not steal and (thou) stealest: thou, that sayest man should not commit adultery, (thou) committest adultery."[70] "Physician, heal thyself." How, as S. Gregory says, can a priest heal others, "with an ulcer in his own face"?[71] A priest will be *aut forma gregis aut fabula*: either the pattern or the by-word. *Ira est non gratia cum quis ponitur supra ventum nullas habens radices in soliditate virtutum.* [72] What measure of spiritual perfection, what measure of sanctity, is proportioned to such an office, to such a charge, to such a responsibility? "Therefore the sanctity of the priest ought to be a sanctity not common to all, but singular in degree: a sanctity which seeks only the things of Christ: a sanctity which has its conversation in heaven: a sanctity which offers itself as an oblation and sacrifice to God in the odour of sweetness: a sanctity by which the priest becomes a fountain of light, of benediction, of merit, and of eternal life to souls: a sanctity which is an example to the faithful in word, in conversation, in charity, in faith, in chastity."[73]

---

[70] Rom ii. 17-22.

[71] Reg. Past. P. i. c. ix.

[72] Petri Bles. *Canon Episcopalis*, Opp. p. 450, 2.

[73] *Parvum Speculum Sacerdotis*, cap. vii. p. 250.

These three relations of the priest are motives to aspire towards the highest conformity to our Divine Master, and to the closest union with Him. And these motives are not only prompted by generosity, gratitude, and love — that is, by the law of liberty — but they contain in themselves, and they impose upon the priest, duties of obligation to which we will now go on.

CHAPTER IV.

THE OBLIGATIONS TO SANCTITY IN THE PRIESTHOOD.

Hitherto we have dwelt upon the priesthood as invested with the greatest power ever bestowed by God on man. This alone would suffice to show that it demands of the priest — not a proportionate consecration of all his living powers, for that is impossible — but an entire oblation of himself. It shows also that with the priesthood a proportionate grace, adequate for the discharge of all his duties, is given to the priest. This alone would suffice to show that the state of the priesthood is the highest in its powers, obligations, and grace: and that it is the state of perfection instituted by our Divine Lord to be the light of the world, and the salt of the earth.

We have seen, also, that the priesthood is one; and that every priest shares it because he partakes in the priesthood of the Incarnate Son; that he is thereby conformed to Him, and that this conformity or configuration is impressed by an indelible character upon the soul.

What more stringent obligations to perfection can be found than these divine participations demand?

We have further seen that a priest is bound by three relations, of which each one demands the perfection of purity, charity, and humility. He is related, first, by manifold duties to his Divine Master; secondly, to His sacramental Presence; and thirdly, to the members of His mystical Body over whom he exercises a jurisdiction of life or of death.

What sanctity can be conceived proportionate to such relations of intimacy, trust, and responsibility between the priest and his Divine Master?

1. It is theologically certain that interior spiritual perfection is a pre-requisite condition to receiving sacred Orders. S. Alphonsus declares that this is the judgment of all Fathers and Doctors with one voice.[74]

---

[74] S. Gregory of Nazianzum may be taken as an example. He describes the spiritual perfection required before ordination to the priesthood in these words: "I, then, knowing these things, and that no one is worthy of the great God, and of the sacrifice, and of the High Priest who has not first offered himself to God a living and holy sacrifice, and shown forth the reasonable and acceptable service, and offered to God the sacrifice of praise, and a contrite heart, which is the only sacrifice demanded of us by the Giver of all things, how should I (without these things) dare to offer to Him the outward antitype of these great mysteries; or how put on the name and habit of a priest before (my) hands be consecrated by holy works; before my eyes are accustomed healthily to behold the creature, and to worship the Creator alone; . . . before my feet be planted upon the rock, perfect as the hart's, and all my ways be directed according to God, neither deviating in any degree nor at all (from Him); before every member become a weapon of justice, all dead works being cast off, swallowed up of life and giving place to the Spirit?"— Orat. ii. c. xcv. tom. i. pp. 56, 57.
S. Gregory then requires of the candidate for the priesthood before ordination an oblation of himself, the service of his reason and will, a spirit of praise and of contrition, holiness of life, separation from creatures, adoration of the Creator, stability in grace, sanctification of all our members, mortification of passions, and the reign of the Holy Ghost in

There are two kinds of men who are called by our Lord to be His priests. The first are the innocent, who, like S. John, S. Philip, and S. Charles, grew up from their earliest consciousness in sanctifying grace and interior perfection. The second are the penitent, as S. Paul, who had persecuted the name of Jesus; S. Augustine, who had wandered early from the divine law; S. Thomas of Canterbury, who had been immersed in the world without falling from God, and yet with many imperfections. The antecedents of these two kinds are widely unlike, but their end is one and the same. They come up to the altar by paths far apart; but they meet before it in one heart and mind, conformed to the perfection of the Great High Priest.

This interior spiritual perfection consists not in a sinless state — for who is without sin? — but first, in such a freedom from the power of sin that they would willingly die rather than commit a mortal sin; and next, in such a fear and aversion from all sin that they would willingly suffer any pain or loss rather than offend God by a wilful venial sin; and thirdly, by a glad and deliberate choice of a life in the spirit of poverty, humility, labour, and the Cross — that is, the lot of their Divine Master; so

---

the soul.
And again: "This, too, I know, that under the law it was ordained that no priest blemished in the body, or while separated from the sacrifices, could offer the perfect oblations, but the perfect (τελειουσ) only— a symbol, as I judge, of the perfection of the soul." — Orat. ii. c. xciv. tom. i. p. 56.

that, even if they could enjoy the world and yet be saved, they would choose to be conformed to Him in His mental sorrows, and in the manifold ways of His Cross. Such a state, with a reign of the love of God and of souls, even though the impetuosities of sudden infirmity and the indeliberate movements and faults of nature still remain, is the interior spiritual perfection which the Fathers and Doctors require of those who come to be ordained to the priesthood.

S. Alphonsus says that they all hold that the state of sanctifying grace is not sufficient for ordination. But all who are in a state of sanctifying grace are united with God. Union with God, therefore, is not enough for the priesthood. Union with God — that is, a freedom from mortal sin — is, indeed, enough for Communion. No such Communion is bad; but such a Communion is not therefore devout, and may be on the brink of danger. If such, without sin, may be the state of faithful, such cannot be the state of a priest who consecrates and consumes the Body and Blood of Jesus Christ, and distributes the Bread of Life to others. The world has sunk so low that some think that only a more than common goodness is required as a sufficient condition for a priest: that is, that a priest, who has the priesthood and character of the Son of God, and is surrounded by all the supernatural relations of which we have spoken, must, indeed, be more than commonly good, but may be on the common level of all other men, of whom not one of these divine and pre-eminent obligations can be affirmed. Such perfunctory and professional goodness is hardly the mark of the disciple of a Lord who was crucified.

The Episcopate has been defined as "the order which has spiritual power to rule and to propagate the Church of God by the perpetuity of sacred ordination."[75] The chief office, therefore, of the Bishop is to choose out, to try, to train, and so make perfect, the youths who are to be admitted to the priesthood. From twelve years old, as the Council of Trent orders, they should be trained in the seminary, already admitted to the clerical state by tonsure. From twelve to twenty-four they are under the eye and hand of the Bishop, for, though others work under him, he is so the head and source of their training that a Council of Toledo calls the seminary *Episcopalis praesentia*. So far as human discernment can reach, such youths grow up in grace to interior spiritual perfection. The others who come at the ninth or the eleventh hour must still ascend by the seven steps which lead to the altar. If the time of their training is shorter, not less is required of them — rather more is exacted of them; and until the same interior spiritual perfection is reached, they slowly ascend towards the Holy Sacrifice. The fervour of conversion and the reparation of penance accomplishes in them in briefer time what the innocence of those who have never sorrowed for sin perhaps more slowly reaches. The fervour of S. Paul and of S. Augustine spring from the *saevitia in seipsum* — the wrath against themselves which is the perfection of penance. S. Gregory says that a soldier who has given way at the outset of the battle will often turn again and fight more heroically than those who have never

---

[75] Ferrante, *Elementa Juris Can.* p. 39.

wavered. But the innocent and the penitent must both attain interior spiritual perfection before they kneel for the laying on of the hands which impress on them the character of the Eternal Priesthood.

It is moreover to be always borne in mind that a priest is ordained *ad exercendam perfectionem* — that is, not only to be perfect, but by his own life, and by the action and influence of his life in word and deed on others, to exhibit and to impress on them the perfection of our Divine Lord. The priesthood was ordained to perpetuate three things: the witness for the truths of faith, the administration of the Sacraments of grace, and the mind of Jesus Christ. The mind of Jesus Christ is not to be manifested in words only, but in the living power of a mind conformed to His. "Ye are the light of the world" signifies that, as light manifests itself by its own radiance, so the priest must shine by the light of a holy life revealing a holy mind. "Ye are the salt of the earth" signifies the personal possession of the sanctity which resists corruption, and the communicating of the same resistance to others by contact and influence. To exercise perfection, then, is to act according to the rule and spirit of perfection: to act, to speak, to judge, to think as the perfect man would. To exercise perfection is to be and to do what is perfect in the personal and priestly life in piety, humility, charity, self-denial. To exercise is to elicit, to exert, to effect. It is a word of power and energy, of self-command and inward force issuing in outward results.

Schoolmen have disputed whether a priest, who is himself imperfect, could exercise perfection. It is, indeed, an axiom: *Extra statum perfectionis perfecti multi, intra statum perfectionis multi imperfecti*. But S. Augustine says, *Nemo potest dare quod non habet*.

If it be said that Judas preached the kingdom of God; that truth has its own vital power; that even mortal sin in the priest does not hinder the *opus operatum* — that is, the grace of the Sacraments; that any priest may teach others to be humble, charitable, pure, and pious; that if the ground be good and the seed good, no matter what be the hand that sows it — all this may be true — the love and compassion of our Lord for souls will not suffer the faithful to be defrauded by bad priests, or even by imperfect priests who have entered the priesthood without the interior spiritual perfection needed for ordination, or, having entered rightly, have afterwards lost it. All this may be true; but this is not *exercere perfectionem*. Such a priest does not exercise or put forth what he does not possess; but the grace and truth which came by Jesus Christ work their own effects through him, to his own condemnation. They work like *gratiae gratis datae*, which are given for the sanctification of others, but do not sanctify those by whom they are dispensed. This is not the doctrine of the Church: neither is the priesthood of our Divine Master a *gratia gratis data*. It is a Sacrament which sanctifies those who receive it, and bestows on them a perennial and inexhaustible sacramental grace for its faithful and fruitful exercise.

This is precisely expressed in the Pontifical. In the first preface for the ordination of priests the Bishop warns the candidates that they must ascend to so high a grade as the priesthood with great fear, and must take heed to possess "heavenly wisdom, moral integrity, and a mature observance of justice;" it further says that our Lord, in choosing out the seventy-two and sending them out to preach before Him, taught us both by word and deed that the ministers of His Church ought to be perfect in the twofold love of God and man, and founded in virtue. He charges them to preserve in their morals the integrity of a chaste and holy life. And finally, he commands them as follows: "Realise what you are now doing; imitate (the sanctity) with which you are charged, that in celebrating the mystery of the Lord's death you may mortify all vices and lusts in your members. Let your doctrine be the spiritual medicine of the people of God. Let the odour of your life be the delight of the Church of Christ, that by preaching and by example you may edify the house that is the family of God."

In the second preface the Bishop further prays: "Renew in them the spirit of holiness, that they may receive of Thee the office of the second dignity, and may, by the example of their conversation, impose a rule of moral life. May they be prudent fellow-workers with us; may the pattern of all justice shine forth in them."[76]

In like manner the Council of Trent orders that all clerics shall visibly show in their lives, by their dress, their gesture, their gait, their words, and in all other things, nothing but gravity, modesty, and piety, and that they avoid even lighter faults which in them would be great; so that "their actions shall inspire all with veneration."[77] These words

---

[76] Pontif. Rom. in Ordinatione Presbyteri.
[77] Sess. xxii. De Ref. cap. i.

express the exercise of perfection in its fullest sense, which is twofold — first, that the priest shall show the practice of perfect charity in his own life; and next, that he diffuse the same by impressing the same law of charity upon others.

Lastly, without more words, it must he self-evident that the interior spiritual perfection required as a condition to ordination, and therefore as an essential condition to the exercise of perfection upon others, imposes on the priest after ordination the strictest obligation to persevere by all means necessary in that perfect life.

Happy is the priest who perseveres in the self-oblation made on the day when he was ordained: unhappy above all men is the priest who falls from it. To such may be said the divine and terrible words: "I have somewhat against thee because thou hast left thy first charity;"[78] or, "I would thou wert cold or hot; but because thou art lukewarm, and neither cold nor hot, I will begin to vomit thee out of My mouth;"[79] or even, "Thou hast the name of being alive, and thou art dead."[80] If the state of the priesthood were the state *perfectionis adquirendae*, such a man might more easily regain his fervour. But it is a state *perfectionis exercendae, conservandae, et amplius augmentandae.* He has already received the greatest vocation, next after the divine maternity of Mary and the foster-fatherhood of Joseph, ever bestowed on man: and with it the greatest grace, because proportionate to that

---

[78] Apoc. ii. 4
[79] Ibid. iii. 15,16
[80] Ibid. iii. 1.

vocation. S. Paul says to every one of us, "Be thou an example of the faithful in word, in conversation, in charity, in faith, in chastity. Neglect not the grace that is in thee, which was given thee by prophecy, with imposition of the hands of the priesthood. Meditate upon these things: be wholly in these things — *haec meditare, in his esto*: that thy proficiency (that is, thy growth in sanctity) may be manifest to all. Take heed to thyself and to doctrine: be earnest in them, for in doing this thou shalt both save thyself, and them that hear thee."[81] In this we see the *exercitium perfectionis in se, et in alios*, the exercise of personal and of pastoral perfection, first in his own life, and next in his actions upon his flock. *Ut perfectus sit homo Dei.*[82]

    The last three chapters and the present have all been directed to one end, namely, to show by how many and by how stringent obligations a priest is bound to the life of perfection. The notion of obligation has been so identified with laws, canons, vows, and contracts that, if these cannot be shown to exist, no obligation is supposed to exist. It is true that all laws, canons, vows, and contracts lay obligations upon those who are subject to them. But all obligations are not by laws, nor by canons, nor by vows, nor by contracts. There are obligations distinct from and anterior to all these bonds. Faith, hope, charity, contrition, piety, all bind the soul by the most persuasive and constraining obligations. The law of liberty binds by love, gratitude, and generosity. Compared with these it may be said all bonds are as the letter that may kill to the spirit

---

[81] 1 S. Tim. iv. 12-16.
[82] 2 S. Tim. iii. 17.

which gives life. These bonds of Jesus Christ are upon all His disciples, and emphatically upon His priests. Upon them are all the obligations arising from their participation in His eternal office, in the sacerdotal character, in their special configuration to their Divine Master, in the divine powers of consecration and absolution: in their personal relations to Jesus, to His sacramental Presence, to His mystical Body. If these things do not demand of men aspiring to be priests interior spiritual perfection before their hands are anointed for the Holy Sacrifice, and the yoke of the Lord is laid upon their shoulder, what has God ever ordained, or the heart of man ever conceived, to bind men to perfection?

CHAPTER V.

THE INSTRUMENTAL MEANS OF PERFECTION.

S. Paul says: "We know that to them that love God all things work together unto good to such as, according to His purpose, are called to he Saints. For whom He foreknew He also predestinated to he made conformable to the image of His son, that He might be the first-born amongst many brethren. And whom He predestinated, them He also called. And whom He called, them He also justified. And whom He justified, them He also glorified:"[83] that is, He laid upon them the glory of the adoption as sons of God. Such is the end of our predestination as Christians; and the means to that end are vocation, justification, and adoption. And these means, with the graces of the Holy Ghost that are attached to them, are proportionate and adequate to the attainment of conformity to the Son of God, both in this life and in eternity. The works of God never fail on His part. If they fail, they are frustrated on our part. Grace enough is given to every regenerate soul to attain sanctity. All are called to be Saints: not, indeed; in the same measure or degree; for "star differeth from star in glory." The paths and vocations of men are beyond all number in their measures and diversities; but to each is given grace adequate to the attainment of the end to which he is called, and the circumstances of the path by which he is to attain it.

---

[83] Rom. viii. 28-30.

This sovereign law of the Holy Ghost is expressed by S. Bernardine of Sienna in words well known.[84]

Of all those who are predestinated to be conformed to the image of Jesus Christ, they come first who share His priesthood and character. They are called to be like Him, that they may be the representatives of His person, and the images of His mind. To them, therefore, are given all proportionate and adequate means of the closest conformity to Him.

The means given to priests for this end are of two kinds: those that are of a general, and those that are of a special, nature. At present, we will keep to those which are general, and leave the special means, merely naming them, for a future chapter.

The general means are three: first, the sacramental grace of priesthood; secondly, the exercise of the priesthood; and thirdly, the exercise of the pastoral office.

1. The first means to sacerdotal perfection is the sacramental grace of the priesthood. Sometimes it is said to be attached to the character; sometimes to flow from it. Every Sacrament confers sanctifying grace; but as each is ordained for a distinct end, a

---

[84] "Omnium singularium gratiarum alicui rationabili creaturae communicatarum generalis regula est quod quandocunque divina gratia eligit aliquem ad aliquam gratiam singularem, seu ad aliquem sublimem statum, omnia charismata donet, quae illi personae sic electo et ejus offcio necessaria sunt, atque illam copiose decorant," — Serm. de S. Joseph, tom. iv. p. 231.

special grace is given by each for the distinct end of each. S. Thomas describes it as follows: "As the virtues and gifts add, beyond the grace commonly so called, a certain perfection ordained determinately to the acts proper to the powers (of the soul); so the sacramental grace adds, beyond the grace commonly so called, and beyond the virtues and gifts, a divine help, *auxilium divinum,* for the attainment of the end of the Sacrament"[85] But this divine help is not given once for all, but initially, as the opening of a spring from which a stream flows and multiplies itself into manifold *auxilia* or helps in time of need, trial, danger, or temptation.

It is, therefore, of faith not only that in ordination sanctifying grace — unless a bar be put by the unworthiness of the man — proportionate to the sacerdotal state is given; but also that a distinct and special divine help, adequate, continuous, and manifold, enabling the priest to fulfil all the obligations of his priesthood. A priest has three characters, and therefore a threefold sacramental grace: as a son, a soldier, and a priest. These divine helps never fail on God's part. If there be failure, it is the priest that fails. It is his own sin, or his own slackness, or his own sloth, or his own insensibility to the divine helps that are urging and empowering him for the duty or the aspiration from which he shrinks. S. Paul answers his own question, "For these things who is sufficient?" by saying, "I can do all things through Him strengthening me."

It is of divine faith that God does not command impossibilities. And also that, to him that

---

[85] *Summa Theol.* P. iii. q. lxii. a. 2.

uses the grace he has, more grace is given. The priesthood is indeed a high estate and an arduous work. Men may shrink from it laudably, from humility, self-mistrust, and holy fear. But when the indelible character has been once impressed upon them, to waver and to doubt is like Peter upon the sea when the winds and waves were boisterous. Our Lord in him rebukes our cowardice: "thou of little faith, wherefore didst thou doubt?" And these words ought to be forever in our ears. If we begin to sink it is because we have begun to doubt. And then we begin to look here and there, backwards and forwards, and to think that safety and rest and sanctity is to be found in this state and the other, and anywhere but in our own. This is want of humble faith. If we would only use the grace we have we should never fail; and in using it the grace would be increased, or doubled, or multiplied tenfold in reward of humility and fidelity, and simple trust in our Divine Master. No man has so many talents to trade with till his Master comes again as a priest. And no man can therefore lay up for himself so great a reward. Of our Blessed Mother alone it can be said that she corresponded with every light and inspiration and grace of the Holy Ghost; and that promptly and adequately, so that the increase of her grace cannot be measured, and is called an immensity. But every priest, though far below Her because of our original sin and faults and falls, and of our tardy and inadequate correspondence with our great and innumerable graces — every priest may gain and store up in himself a great depth of sanctification, always increasing through life, and accumulating more and more unto the end.

If it should so happen that any man by sin or sloth barred the grace of his ordination at the outset of his life, by true conversion to God the grace which sin had bound may yet revive. If in the course of his life he should lose his fervour, or even his spiritual life, the Sacrament of penance will restore him to grace, and by contrition the sacramental grace may yet revive. Who, then, needs to despair? Hope honours our Divine Lord. Let us hope greatly, strongly, and with perseverance to the end.

2. But, secondly, the priesthood itself is a source of sanctification to the priest. It is a restraint and a guard and a shelter against the world. It is a motive and a measure of aspiration. It is a constant impulse after a higher degree of union with God. A priest is set apart for God's greatest glory; and on all his sacerdotal life, as on the vessels of the Temple, is written *Sanctificatus Domino.* [86] To this also his personal actions ought to correspond. The words of the Psalmist ought to be expressly true in the mouth of a priest. "One thing I have asked of the Lord, that will I seek after, that I may dwell in the house of the Lord all the days of my life: that I may see the delight of the Lord, and may visit His temple; for He hath hidden me in His tabernacle."[87] The "one thing" of a priest's life is to dwell near our Lord on the altar, to bear the key of the tabernacle, and to be as a disciple ad *latus Domini* — by the side of his Lord. The title "*Alter Christus*" is both a joy and a rebuke. If we be identified with our Lord He will dwell in us and reign in us. "The charity of Christ urgeth us" — that is, His love to us urges us to love

---

[86] Zach. xiv. 21.
[87] Ps. xxvi. 4-6.

Him, to serve Him with all our inward life; for He died for us to this end — "that we should no longer live unto ourselves." "With Christ I am nailed to the Cross; and I live, now not I, but Christ liveth in me."[88]

If the presence of Jesus penetrates throughout the soul; if it pervades the intellect, the will, the affections, He lives in us, and we, by Him, should live a supernatural life. All our freedom would still be perfect, but His mind and His inspiration would reign over us. We should think His thoughts, speak His words, do His acts. What a multitude of sweetness it would bring into our whole life if we, as priests, could say, "I live, not I, but Christ liveth in me." The world would have nothing in us: we should neither seek it nor fear it. The consciousness of our predestination and vocation, and justification and adoption, and of our second and higher vocation to be in a special manner and measure conformed to the image of the Son by partaking of His priesthood, would be a perpetual motive to all perfection.

3. Lastly, the pastoral office also is in itself a discipline of perfection. For, first of all, it is a life of abnegation of self. A pastor has as many obediences to fulfil as he has souls to serve. The good and the evil, the sick and the whole, the young and the old, the wise and the foolish, the worldly and the unworldly — who are not always wise — the penitent and the impenitent, the converting and the unconverted, the lapsed and the relapsed, the obdurate and the defiant, all must be watched over.

---

[88] Gal. ii. 19,20.

None may be neglected — still less cast off — always, at all times, and in all ways possible. S. Philip used to say that a priest should have no time of his own, and that many of his most consoling conversions came to him out of hours, at unseasonable moments. If he had sent them away because they came out of time, or at suppertime, and the like, they might have been lost. Then again the trials of temper, patience, and self-control in bearing with the strange and inconsiderate minds that come to him; and the demands made upon his strength and endurance day and night in the calls of the sick and dying, coming often one after another when for a moment he has gone to rest; the weary and continual importunities of people and of letters till the sound of the bell or the knock at the door is a constant foreboding too surely fulfilled: all these things make a pastor's life as wearisome and, strange to say, as isolated as if he were in the desert. No sackcloth so mortifies the body as this life of perpetual self-abnegation mortifies the will. But when the will is mortified the servant is like his Master, and his Master is the exemplar of all perfection. "Si ergo dilectionis est testimonium cura pastionis, quisquis virtutibus pollens gregem Dei renuit pascere, pastorem summum convincitur non amare."[89]

To this must be added that the pastor's office is the highest discipline of charity; and charity is the perfection of God and man. It was charity that moved him to become a pastor, and charity binds him to give his life for his flock. Between the beginning and the ending of his life charity is the

---

[89] S. Greg, in Reg. Past. P. i. c. v.

urgent motive which constrains, sustains, and spends all his living powers. He knows himself to be *vicarius charitatis Christi*. Every action of a faithful pastor is prompted habitually, virtually, or actually by charity. And in every action, from the greatest to the least, as charity is elicited into act, it is augmented by an increase poured out into the heart by the Holy Ghost, the charity of God. "God is charity, and he that abideth in charity abideth in God and God in him."[90] But where God abides there is sanctity, for though charity and sanctity are distinct, they are inseparable, coming and going, growing or lessening in intensity together, like light and heat, which are never parted.

We might draw out this in other details as in humility, purity, piety, generosity, and the like, which are in continual exercise and in continual increase in the life of priests and pastors. But mortification and charity are the two conditions of perfection; and no more words are needed to show that they are called forth into the fullest exercise by the demands of a priestly and pastoral life.

As to the other means of perfection, it will be enough now to enumerate them, because they will come back hereafter on our attention.

First is the law and obligation of chastity, with all its safeguards and sanctities.

Secondly, the life and spirit of poverty which binds a priest in his ecclesiastical revenues, and counsels a pastor with a peremptory voice, in the

---

[90] 1 S. John iv.16.

administration of any patrimony he may possess.

Thirdly is obedience to the Church, to his Bishop, to law, to discipline, to the living voice of authority, which may be as minute and far spreading as any can desire if they have the will to obey.

These three obligations are instrumental means of perfection. To them must be added:

Fourthly, the habit of prayer and meditation, which is the habit of contemplation.

Fifthly, the daily Mass, with its preparation and thanksgiving, and the manifold relations of the priest to the Blessed Sacrament, distributing the Bread of Life to his flock in benedictions, processions, expositions, and in personal visits to the presence of our Divine Lord.

Sixthly, in the confessional. The priest who is faithful and patient as a father, a physician, and a judge of souls, gains more in the living histories of sin and sorrow, contrition and conversion, sanctity and perfection in the confessional, than from all the books upon his shelves.

Seventhly, in the preaching of the Word of God, to which daily meditation and study of Holy Scripture are vitally necessary. S. Augustine says "that a man will preach so much the more or so much the less wisely as be shall have made more or less progress in Holy Scripture."[91]

---

[91] *De Doct. Christ.* lib. iv. 5.

Eighthly, in his seven visits to the heavenly court in the daily Divine Office.

Ninthly, in the rule of life given to him and wrought into him in the seminary, which, in outline at least, has become a second nature, directing, constraining, counselling, and ordering his life in its union with God.

Lastly, in the law of liberty, the highest and most constraining of all obligations, to which we will return hereafter.

With such abundant means of confirming himself in the interior spiritual perfection in which he was ordained, and of attaining continually a nearer conformity to the mind and life of his Master, no priest can fail of any degree of humility, charity, and sanctity, except through his own fault. God has done for us more than we could ask or think. And "the gifts and the calling of God are without repentance"[92] — that is, there is no change of mind or purpose towards His priests, whom He has chosen to be His representatives, and to be, like Himself, "the light of the world" and "the salt of the earth."

---

[92] Rom. xi. 29.

CHAPTER VI.

THE END OF THE PRIEST.

The end of man is the glory of God. The end of a Christian is the greater glory of God. The end of a priest is the greatest glory of God.

1. The greatest work of God in the six days of Creation was man. S. Paul says that "the woman is the glory of the man;" but that "man is the image and glory of God."[93] The works of God arose in an ascending scale from the creation of the light to the inorganic and inanimate creatures, and from these to the organic and animate, and from these again to the rational. There was nothing higher than man under God except the holy Angels, pure, spiritual intelligences, simple and immortal, sinless and resplendent, sanctified and illuminated by the Holy Ghost. Man was made a little lower than the angels, because his spiritual nature was clothed in a body taken from the slime and dust of the earth, and subject, therefore, to the sinless imperfections of an earthly nature. Nevertheless, he was the image of God. His memory, intelligence, and will are an image of the three co-equal and indivisible Persons of the ever-blessed Trinity. He was, therefore, the glory of God, in a sense beyond all other creatures, for no other could render to God the λογικην λατρειαν, the *obsequium rationabile*, the obedience of reason and of faith, and serve Him as a son and as a friend.

---

[93] 1 Cor. xi. 7.

And man, when created, was crowned with glory and honour. His nature was itself his glory, for it reflected the perfections of God. The light of his reason was his crown, radiant with the knowledge of God and of himself. And God set him over all the works of His hands. He gave him sovereignty and lordship — a dominion of use and of enjoyment held by divine grant, and limited by the law of the divine perfections. This warrants no excess beyond the intentions and conditions of the dominion which God delegated to man.

Man was, then, the first-fruits of the old creation.

2. But what the first Adam was among creatures the second Adam is among men. The first man was only man in stature and perfection, united indeed with God by the indwelling of the Holy Ghost; but in no way above or beyond the dimensions of manhood. The second Man is God Incarnate, and our manhood in Him is deified. It was humanity in all things such as ours, yet without sin, taken of the substance of a sinless Mother, pure and blessed as the virgin earth before sin entered. The Incarnation was the new creation of God. S. Paul so writes: "God, who commanded the light to shine out of darkness, hath shined in our hearts to give the light of the knowledge of the glory of God, in the face of Jesus Christ."[94] He was, in a twofold fulness, the image of God. He was the eternal Image of the Father as God; and the reflected Image of God as man. The original and the likeness in Him were united; and the glory of His countenance is the

---

[94] 2 Cor. iv. 6.

Light of the World. "God, who at sundry times and in divers manners spoke in times past to the Fathers, by the Prophets, last of all, in these days hath spoken to us by His Son, whom He hath appointed Heir of all things, by whom also He made the world."[95] All the lights of nature and of reason, and of continual revelation by prophets and seers ascended into the full and final revelation of God by Jesus Christ, "the brightness of His glory, and the figure of His substance." [96] All holiness, justice, wisdom, mercy, humility, charity, sympathy, and tenderness were revealed in the person of Jesus Christ.

Jesus Christ, therefore, is the first-fruits of the new creation.

3. S. James writes: "Of His own will hath He begotten us by the word of truth, that we might be some beginning of His creatures;"[97] that is to say, those who are born again of water and the Holy Ghost are the first-fruits among the nations. The word απαρχη is as the beginning of the harvest, when the first sheaf, reaped and bound, was lifted up before the Lord as the first-fruits of the field.[98] So among the nations is the Body of Christ the fellowship of the regenerate, who, by a new birth, have risen from spiritual death to spiritual life, and are thereby partakers of immortality. They are members of a Divine Head, who is "the first-fruits of

---

[95] Heb. i. 1,2.
[96] Ibid. i. 3.
[97] S. James i. 18.
[98] Levit. xxiii. 10,11.

them that slept;"[99] and in Him also they are risen, and have become partakers of the powers of the world to come.[100] S. Paul says that we have "the first-fruits of the spirit."[101] S. Peter describes the Christian people as "a chosen generation, a kingly priesthood, a holy nation, a purchased people," whose office in the world is "to declare His virtues who hath called us out of darkness into His marvellous light."[102] And again we are made "the first-fruits to God and to the Lamb"[103] — that is, for the greater glory of God.

If, then, the regenerate are the first-fruits of the world, the priests of Jesus Christ are the first-fruits of the regenerate. If the first-fruits are for the greater glory of God, the first-fruits of the first-fruits must be for His greatest glory. To be chosen out from the chosen people, the elect of the elect; to be partakers of the priesthood of the Incarnate Son, of His character and of His powers; to be the visible witnesses of His mind and of His perfection; to be *aliorum perfectores*; to be set to make others perfect; to be consecrated to offer Him continually as the Victim for the sins of the world; and to offer ourselves in union with Him to God; and, moreover, to offer ourselves to Him for the work He has laid upon us; beyond this, what is there revealed for the glory of God except the eternal service and perfection of the heavenly court? A priest is set to continue the work of his Master. But the work of his

---

[99] 1 Cor. XV. 20.
[100] Heb. vi. 5.
[101] Rom. viii. 23
[102] 1 S. Pet. ii. 9.
[103] Apoc. xiv. 4.

Master was to save and to sanctify mankind. He is chosen and called and consecrated to make visible and sensible the life, the mind, the Word, and the will of Jesus Christ. S. Bernard says: "Feed (the flock) by thy mind, by thy lips, by thy works, by thy spirit of prayer, by the exhortation of thy words, by the example of all thine actions." When our Lord said, "As My Father hath sent Me, so send I you," He meant that His priests should perpetuate in the world not only His truth and His Holy Sacraments, but His own mind, and likeness, and life. And for this He has given us all the necessary means. He chose and taught and trained and assimilated His Apostles to Himself by direct and immediate action. He chooses, calls, and conforms His priests to Himself now no less than in the beginning, though His action be mediate by the divine tradition, and by the action of His mystical Body edifying itself in charity. Dionysius the Areopagite, whosoever he be, says: "He who speaks of a priest speaks of a man most august, and altogether divine, and most skilled in the whole sacred science,"[104] that is, of God. S. Ignatius calls the priest "the culminating point of all goodness among men."[105]

This, then, is an axiom in the law and spirit of the sacerdotal life: that a priest is predestined for the greatest glory of God.

From this, again, it follows that the words of S. Paul ought to be in the heart of every priest: "I count all things loss for the excellent knowledge of Jesus Christ my Lord, for whom I have suffered the

---

[104] De Coelest. Hier. cap. i.

[105] Ep. ad Smyrn. recensio longior, c. ix.

loss of all things, and count them but as dung that I may gain Christ;" "that I may know Him and the power of His resurrection, and the fellowship of His sufferings, being made conformable to His death: if by any means I may attain to the resurrection which is from the dead. Not as though I had already attained, or were already perfect; but I follow after, if I may by any means apprehend wherein I am also apprehended by Christ Jesus. Brethren, I do not count myself to have apprehended. But one thing I do: forgetting the things that are behind, and stretching forth myself to those that are before, I press toward the mark to the prize of the supernal vocation in Christ Jesus."[106] These words of the Holy Ghost express the aim, aspiration, and effort of a faithful priest, always pressing upwards, and always ascending higher and higher in the life of God — the heavenly life of knowledge and power, of the Cross, and of conformity to the Son of God. No words can be added to these without lessening their constraining force. There is no degree of sanctity or perfection to which a priest ought not to aspire. To aim at any mark or measure below the highest is to fall short of our vocation. "Not to advance in virtue, nor out of our old selves to be made new, but to linger in the same state, we account to be a vice."[107] S. Gregory of Nyssa says: "Let no one complain at seeing the liability of nature to change, but let him be always changing himself for the better, and being transformed from glory to glory, becoming better by daily growth, never thinking that he has attained the bounds of perfection. For this is truly perfection: never to

---

[106] Philip, iii. 8-14.
[107] S. Greg. Naz. Orat. iv. § 124, tom. i. p. 147.

stand still in the growth towards what is more perfect, nor to fix any limit to perfection."[108] S. Bernard also says: "Jacob saw angels on the ladder ascending and descending. Did he see any standing still or sitting? It is not possible to stand hanging on a frail ladder, nor in the uncertainty of this mortal life can anything abide. We have not here an abiding city, but we are seeking one to come. Ascend or descend you must. No man is certain that he is good who does not desire to be better; and where you begin to be unwilling to become better, there you begin to cease to be good." And if this warning be true of all Christians, how peremptory is the warning to all priests. He says again, *Solus Deus melior se ipso esse non vult, quia non valet.*[109]

If such be our predestination, what is our state?

1. Of a sinful priest no words are needed. Since the fall of the angels there was nothing ever so hideous as the fall of Judas, and since the fall of Judas nothing so full of dread as the fall of a priest. *Mane eras stella rutilans: vespere conversus es in carbonem.* In the morning, like a star in the brightness of purity: at evening, black and dead as a coal. And this may be not only by sins of the flesh — which to the angels were impossible — but of the spirit, such as the sins against charity, piety, and humility. The sin of Judas was, so far as is written, a spiritual sin, ending in the sale and the betrayal of His Divine Lord. We are not safe from mortal sin by being only chaste and pure. S. Jerome says: *Perfidus Judaeus,*

---

[108] S. Greg. Nyss. *Orat. de Perfect. Christ,* tom. i. p. 298.
[109] S. Bernard, Epist. xci. 2, 3, tom. i. p. 265.

perfidus Christianus, ille de latere, iste de calice sanguinem Christi fundit.

2. Of a worldly priest little need be said. If the love of the Father cannot be in him who loves the world, then chastity and purity will not save us; for if the "concupiscence of the eyes" or "the pride of life" be in us, we are dead already: *"nondum apparuit judicium et jam factum est judicium."* [110] The character of the last days is that men shall be "lovers of their own selves," and "lovers of pleasure more than lovers of God." [111] Such priests may be blameless to the eye, but they may love "the things that are their own, and not the things that are Jesus Christ's."[112]

3. Of a lax priest what can be said? The chief signs of laxity are to live without a rule of life; to say the Holy Mass by custom, with little preparation, and little thanksgiving; to be weary of the confessional; to escape it when possible; to be unpunctual and irregular in attendance. Such a priest soon finds himself more at ease in the world than among priests. The habits, tone, talk, and pleasant ways of the world are more to his taste. He lives in a mission-house or a presbytery, but it is not his home. His home is where his heart is, and his heart is in the world. He is ready for any recreation among people of the world or among women, but not always ready for a sickbed, or a sorrowful tale, or for the Divine Office. In laughter he is unchastened, and in sorrow he is cast down. In

---

[110] S. Aug. Tract, xii. in Joan.
[111] 2 S. Tim. iii. 2-4.
[112] Philip, ii. 21.

prudence and circumspection he is unwary and often blind to what all about him see, but he alone cannot or will not perceive. He is fond of money, and glad when oblations and gifts come in.[113] He can give any length of time to the world, and can always find leisure for what he likes. He is a ready talker, and has a turn for satire. He sees the ludicrous in men and things, and is an amusing companion much sought after. This state is not far from lukewarmness, which S. Bernard defines as "brief and rare compunction, sensuous thoughts, obedience without devotion, talk without circumspection." Of these sins he says again, "Let no man say in his heart these things are light. It is no great matter if I should go on in these venial and lesser sins. This is impenitence: this is blasphemy against the Holy Ghost, and without remission."[114] Once more he says: "Do not despise these things because they are little, but fear them because they are many." And the Council of Trent says: "Let priests avoid light faults, which in them are great." A blot upon a layman's coat is hardly seen, but a spot upon a priest's alb is an eyesore to all men.

It would be well for us to renew every day and wheresoever we are the consciousness that we are predestined and consecrated to the greatest glory of God. The life and the measures allowable to the faithful are not allowable to priests. To all

---

[113] "Quis est in vobis, qui claudat ostia, et incendat altare meum gratuito?" — Malachias i. 10.
[114] "Nemo dicat in corde suo, Levia sunt ista, non curo corrigere non est magnum si in his maneam venialibus minimisque peccatis. Hoc est enim dilectissimi, impoenitentia, haec blasphemia in Spiritum Sanctum, blasphemia irremissibilis." — Serm. i. De Sanctis, tom. iii. p. 2066.

men S. Paul says: "Whether ye eat or drink, or whatever ye do, do all to the glory of God." If such be the law of duty for the layman, what is the obligation of the priest?

CHAPTER VII.

THE PRIEST'S DANGERS.

All that has hitherto been said has raised the priest to so high a state that the next thought must be of his dangers. If he should fall, how great that fall would be. To stand upon the pinnacle of the Temple needs a supernatural poise and fidelity not to fall. It is well — it is even necessary — that we should both number and measure the dangers which beset us.

We can all, perhaps, remember with what a sense of holy fear we prepared for our ordination; with what joy and hope we received the indelible character of priesthood; with what disappointment at ourselves we woke up the next morning, or soon after, to find ourselves the same men we were before. This meeting of devout and hopeful aspiration with the cold hard reality of our conscious state came like a sharp withering wind over the first blossoms of a fruit-tree. But the effect of this was wholesome. It roused and warned us even with fear. We then better understood such words as these: "Son of man, I have made thee a watchman to the house of Israel; and thou shalt hear the word out of My mouth, and shall tell it them from Me. If, when I say to the wicked, 'Thou shalt surely die,' thou declare it not to him, nor speak to him that he may be converted from his wicked way and live, the same wicked man shall die in his iniquity, but I will require his blood at thy hand. But if thou give warning to the wicked, and he be not converted from his wickedness and from his evil way, he indeed shall die in his iniquity, but thou hast delivered thy soul." [115] With this commission weighing upon him, the priest fresh from his ordination enters upon his pastoral work. Then begin his dangers. S. John Chrysostom, after speaking of the trials of Bishops and priests, how they are exposed to all tongues and tempers, accusing them of contradictory things, and taking offence whether we will or no, says: "The priesthood requires a great soul; for the priest has many harassing troubles of his own, and has need of innumerable eyes on all sides."[116] This sounds as a warning. Let us look further into it.

1. To a priest who enters for the first time upon the sacerdotal life the first danger is the loss of the supports on which he has so long been resting in the seminary. As in the launching of a ship, when the stays are knocked away it goes down into the water, thenceforward to depend upon its own stability; so a priest, going out from the seminary into the field of his work, has thenceforward to depend under God upon his own steadfastness of will. The order, method, and division of time and of work; the sound of the bell from early morning through the day till the last toll at night; the example and mutual influence and friendship of companions in the same sacred life; and still more, the mature counsel and wise charity of superiors — all these things sustain the watchfulness and perseverance of ecclesiastical students until the day when, invested with the priesthood, they go out from the old familiar walls and the door is closed

---

[115] Ezech. iii. 17-19.
[116] Hom. iii. in *Acta App.* tom. ix. p. 29.

behind them. They are in the wide world; secular as the Apostles were — that is, in the world, for the world's sake, not of it, but at war with it; of all men the least secular, unless they become worldly, and the salt lose its savour. Then they deserve the title in all its extent, and are seculars indeed.

The first danger, then, of a priest sent out into the world is the loss of all surroundings which, until then, gave him support. For the first time he feels his own weight pressing upon him as a burden. He has a painful sense of loneliness and of unlimited liberty. Everything depends upon his own will and choice. His hours, his employments, his duties, even to the hours of his Mass and to his days for confession; his visits, his friends, his relaxations — all are dependent on his own will. It is a liberty which, generously used, turns all things and every day to gold, but if squandered and indulged must end in spiritual poverty, confusion, and peril. For a life of unlimited liberty is encompassed with manifold temptations. The very atmosphere is charged with danger. Few minds are so self-sufficing that they do not crave after human voices and human sympathies. A priest coming out of a seminary needs fellowship, and he often seeks it in society. He does not as yet know the character of those about him, or the reputation of the homes to which he is invited. Before he is aware he is often entangled in relations he would not have chosen, and in invitations which, if he had the courage, he would refuse. People are very hospitable, and pity a priest's loneliness, and like to have him at their tables. Sometimes the best of people are least circumspect and most kindly importunate in their invitations. How shall a young and inexperienced

75

mind hold out against these facilities and allurements to relaxation, unpunctuality, self-indulgence, and dissipation? The whole of a priest's life may be determined by his first outset. He has been in it too short a time either to gain or to buy experience.

2. Another danger in a priest's life arises from the length of time that he has been in it. He came into it in all the first brightness of the character impressed upon him on the day of his ordination. The exercise of his priesthood, if faithful and fervent, would add a growing brightness to his sacerdotal character and life. But soon "the fine gold becomes dim."[117] He is acclimatised to his surroundings. It may be he is placed among older priests who, though good, have become lax and easy-going. His first charity subsides, and the old mind comes up again. He is the same man as he was before; or perhaps the old habit of mind comes back with the force of a reaction. He began by resolving to live up to many counsels of a higher spirit, but he subsides to the level of commandments. His good resolutions are not retracted, but often unfulfilled, and survive as intentions or conditional promises made by himself to himself, with a large latitude and a wide clause as to the possibility of observance. He does not lower his aim, or his standard by any express change of theory, but be moves along a lower level and with less self-reproach as time goes on.

Such a priest may still keep to the letter of his rule of life, and to the times of his horarium, but

---

[117] Lam. iv. 1.

the interior spirit has declined. He does fewer things with an actual intention, many with a virtual intention, but most with only a habitual intention. He never omits his Mass, nor is absent from the confessional, nor neglects a sick call; but the spirit or mind in which all these things are done is lowered. He is punctual and exact from custom, and from a habit which gradually becomes unconscious. In saying the Divine Office much is said without intellectual attention. Psalm after psalm goes by without advertence, and, when said, no verse in it is remembered. The same befalls the mysteries of the Rosary; and even in the Holy Mass distractions spring off from the mementos of the living and of the departed. Thoughts run on like a double consciousness. The material action of the Mass may be faultless, but the intrusive thoughts overpower the perception of the words. So, again, in the confessional he hears with a wandering mind and absolves with distraction. Still more by the bedside of the sick or dying he is mechanically correct in giving the last Sacraments, but without a living word of consolation or strength, or contrition, or confidence. And yet such a priest may be good in heart, exemplary in life; but he is as a well that is dry, or, as S. Jude says, *nubes sine aqua* — a cloud without water. There is no refreshment in him for the weary or for the thirsty, or for those who seek in him the waters of life and consolation and find none.

3. Another danger of a priest is that he has too much to do. Let no one think that a busy life may not be a holy life. The busiest life may be full of piety. Holiness consists not in doing uncommon things, but in doing all common things with an

uncommon fervour. No life was ever more full of work and of its interruptions than the life of our Lord and His Apostles. They were surrounded by the multitude, and "there were many coming and going, and they had not so much as time to eat."[118] Nevertheless, a busy life needs a punctual and sustained habit of prayer. It is neither piety nor charity for a priest to shorten his preparation before Mass or his thanksgiving after it because people are waiting for him. He must first wait upon God, and then he may serve his neighbour. The hour and a half of a priest's Mass is both his own and not his own. It is the first-fruits of his day. They belong to God: he has the *usufruct*, not the *dominium* of them. He cannot alienate them. If any priest do so he will be forced to say at last, *Vineam meam non custodivi*. The palmer-worm and the canker-worm will do their work stealthily, but surely.

The having too much to do often leads to doing nothing well. All things are done in haste and on the surface. There is no time lost which is given to mental prayer and union with God. Every word that proceeds out of such a mind does more than a hundred words uttered from the lips of a man dried up by overwork. The constant overtax of intellectual and bodily activity tends to form a natural, external, and unspiritual character. It betrays itself in the confessional and in preaching. How often we hear it said, "My confessor is a holy man, but he never speaks a word beyond my penance and absolution." And how surely we know from what a superficial source the ready stream of bright, cold, intellectual preaching flows.

---

[118] S. Mark vi. 31.

4. There is yet in a priest's life another danger the reverse of the last; namely, the having too little to do. If, as we have seen, the exercise of the priesthood and of the pastoral office is of itself a means of sanctification, then in the measure in which it is suspended or unexercised the priest must suffer loss. But the loss is not only privative. Not to have a sufficient demand on his powers to call them out into activity is the reason of the inertness and incapacity of many a priest who is capable of great effort and of high attainment. There are two things which bring out into activity the powers that lie hid in men. The one is a great force of will which makes a man independent of external stimulus. The other is the tax which is laid upon him by duty and responsibility. Few have such force of will, and many have little to tax or elicit their powers. Sometimes men who, as students or clerics, promised great works for the Church have been placed by necessity in a sphere so narrow that their powers have had little to call them out. Such a sphere was too limited for their zeal. But in saying this we must not forget the words of S. Charles: that one soul is diocese enough for a Bishop. In counting by number we lose sight of the worth of each single soul, and the reward of saving if it be only one eternal soul. This would give work enough to a priest in the scarcest flock. But this conviction needs much reflection and much force of will. The effect of inactivity on most men is relaxation, and a love of ease. A small mission becomes a Sleepy Hollow, and the priest too often a harmless lotus-eater. First, time is wasted, and then powers waste themselves; as muscles not used grow weak, so the brain and the will grow inert and torpid. A vigorous man will

make his own work. Time never hangs heavy on his hands. He will make work when none is made for him. Priests who have only a handful of souls may become theologians and authors, and may serve the Church more lastingly by their writings than by their activity. Leisure and tranquillity are two necessary conditions for sacred study. And, as S. Augustine said, *Quamobrem otium quaerit charitas veritatis; negotium justum suscipit necessitas charitatis. Quam sarcinam si nullus imponit, percipiendae atque intuendae vacandum est veritati.*[119]

But for this are necessary a love of study, or a constraining conscience, and a resolute will. For the most part good men succumb to any easy life, which, blameless as it may be, is too like to the servant who folded his talent in the napkin. When a man has neither work enough nor study enough to fill his mind, he suffers from monotony, and is restless for change. He is weary of vacancy, and craves for an interest. He finds none at home, and he seeks it abroad. His mind wanders first, and he follows it. His life becomes wasted and dissipated — that is, scattered and squandered, full of weariness and a tediousness in all things, which at last invades even his acts and duties of religion. A priest may be chaste and temperate in all things; but weariness is the descending path which leads to sloth, and sloth is the seventh of the sins which kill the soul. To have too much to do is for most men safer than to have too little.

5. There is still one more danger to which the last directly leads, and that is lukewarmness. It

---

[119] S. Aug. *De Civ. Dei*, lib. xix. c. xix. tom. vii. p. 426.

was to a Bishop our Lord said: "Thou art neither cold nor hot. I would thou wert cold or hot; but because thou art neither cold nor hot I will begin to vomit thee out of My mouth."[120] The rejection is not yet complete, but it is begun; and if the priest does not know himself it must come at last. A lax priest is of all men most to be pitied. When his priesthood ceases to be sweet to him, it becomes first tasteless, and then bitter in the mouth. The perpetual round of the same actions and the same obligations becomes mechanical and automatous. *Sancta sancte*, as the Council of Carthage enjoins. But when holy things cease to be sustaining and refreshing, they are a yoke which galls, and a burden which oppresses. Such priests easily omit Mass, and have no sense of loss.

Still they may preach high doctrines of the spiritual life with as much eloquence as ever. But their heart does not go with their words; and to ears that can hear there is a hollow ring in all they say. Such men will read the lives of the Saints, and desire to be like them. They try and fall short. They retain an intellectual perception of some high standard which is habitually in their mouth till an unconscious intellectual simulation is formed, sometimes with self-deception, which is dangerous; sometimes with conscious unreality, which is worse. Such men grow inwardly hollow. There is a decay at the heart, and a preparation for falling. The words of Isaias are fearful and true: "Therefore shall this iniquity be to you as a breach that falleth, and is found wanting in a high wall; for the destruction thereof shall come on a sudden, when it is not

---

[120] Apoc. iii. 15,16.

looked for." Many a time when a priest has fallen all men have wondered except one or two, who have closely watched him, and his own conscience, which has known the secret of his fall. And when it comes, it is terrible, and sometimes final. The "high wall" comes rushing down in utter ruin; the higher the more hopeless. As the prophet says again: "And it shall be broken small as the potter's vessel is broken all to pieces with mighty breaking; and there shall not a sherd be found of the pieces thereof wherein a little fire may be carried from the hearth, a little water drawn out of the pit."[121] When angels fell they fell for ever; for there was for them no redemption. When a priest falls he may rise again, for his Master is very pitiful. But since Satan fell like lightning from heaven there has been no fall like the fall of a priest.

---

[121] Isaias xxx. 13,14.

CHAPTER VIII.

THE PRIEST'S HELPS.

Sometimes we say, or at least we feel, "If I had known what it is to be a priest I should never have ventured. I have all the dangers of other men, and many that are the perils only of a priest. They are set up on high, and they are set over souls to give account. The world and Satan have special enmity and malice against a priest. What good does my life do me? I am not better than my fathers; and if I fall, my fall will be great, and perhaps irremediable. *Grandis sacerdotis dignitas sed grandis ruina.*" Such thoughts often come by the suggestion of the tempter and the fault of our own hearts. But, unless we play false to ourselves, a truer mind soon asserts itself; and we say, "I have the dangers of other men, but I have graces beyond them all. They have the sacramental grace of sons and of soldiers, but I have also the sacramental grace of a priest." If the dangers of a priest are great, his sacramental grace is greater than his dangers. He has helps both general and special in the exercise of his priesthood, which are more than adequate for every duty, danger, and temptation.

We have already spoken of the general helps of the priesthood, and of the pastoral care: we will now count up the special helps which surround a priest in all his life.

1. First, and above all, is his daily Mass. "When the morning was come, Jesus stood on the

shore." The day begins with the presence of Jesus; the altar is the shore of the Eternal World, and Jesus comes at our word. In the Holy Mass we know Him, and yet our eyes are holden. He is in another form. We cannot see Him; but we know that it is the Lord. He makes ready for us, and gives to us the Bread of Life. If we were to spend a whole life in preparation, one such divine contact with His Presence would be an overpayment of all our prayer and penance and purification of heart.[122] But He comes to us, not once in our life only, but morning by morning. Every day begins with Him. If the first hour of every day were spent in the presence — certain though unseen — of our guardian angel or of our patron Saint, our whole day would be restrained and elevated by it. Familiarity might deaden at last our vivid sense of so near an approach of the supernatural world and we might cease to realise it. But the Holy Mass is more than all this. It is the personal Presence of the Lord of angels and of Saints; and yet, through familiarity with the exceeding condescension of His great humility, we may gradually lose the vividness of our perception. The Council of Trent teaches us that the Presence of Jesus is above the laws and order of nature.[123] He is there, God and Man in personal reality and substance; and we, when we hold the Blessed Sacrament in our hands, are in contact with the Creator, Redeemer, and Sanctifier of the world. The Council says again that He is present, not as in

---

[122] S. Gregory of Nazianzum says: "Extreme old age would not be a long preparation for the priesthood" — Orat. 11. § lxxii.

[123] *Catech. Trid. ad Par.* P. iv. c. 2.

a place, but as He is — a substance.[124] In the divine order there is no time, and place is not. We are in contact with the eternal world; and that contact is real and substantial and personal, both on His side and on ours. We behold Him face to face by the vision of faith. Beyond this there is nothing but the vision of the blessed. After the consecration we are already admitted to it under a veil. *Nobis quoque peccatoribus*, to us sinners also is granted in the Holy Mass a share and a friendship with the Saints and Martyrs in the heavenly court. From the consecration to the Communion we are as truly and more consciously with Him than Cleophas and his companion in the way to Emmaus. And though our eyes are holden our understanding is not. We see Him in another shape; but we know Him while we see Him. And we speak to Him as our Lord, our Master, our Friend; and by an inward speech He answers us in words which it is not in man to utter. His abiding is for a short interval of time, but that brief time encloses an abyss of light and peace. We say Mass morning by morning all our life, but we never reach the end of this mystery of His personal nearness. There is no fixed horizon to the multitude of His sweetness,[125] which expands on every side like the illimitable sea. And yet all its sweetness is hid in the Blessed Sacrament for those who seek Him in holy fear. And before He departs from us for a season, to come again to-morrow, He takes and gives to us His precious Body and Blood as in the guest-chamber, on that last night of farewell, and as at Emmaus, when He vanished out of their sight. He is gone, but in a little while He is to be

---

[124] Ibid. P. ii. c. iv. 36.
[125] Ps. XXX. 20.

found again in the midst of His disciples; as the Council says again that "Jesus, having loved His own while He was in the world, loved them to the end:" "that He might never be absent from His own, gave us, by an inexplicable counsel of His wisdom, a pledge of His love above the order and conditions of nature" [126] — that is, His own perpetual Presence veiled from sight. When the Archangel Raphael departed from Tobias and his son so that they could see him no more, they lay "for three hours prostrate on their faces."[127] What ought to be our thanksgiving after Mass?

If I do not speak of Communion it is because I need not. Every priest knows what no words could tell. We cannot make colour or sweetness visible or sensible to the intelligence alone. Sight and taste only can know. Therefore the Holy Ghost says, "Taste and see that the Lord is sweet."[128] We must taste first and see afterwards; but it is by an internal sight which needs no light, and has no limits of sense. In every Communion we are made flesh of His flesh and bone of His bone; and if our hearts are pure we are made also heart of His Heart, mind of His mind, will of His will, spirit of His spirit. We are not straitened in Him, but in ourselves. If our hearts were prepared as they might and ought to be by contrition and piety, the sacramental grace of even one Communion would suffice to sanctify us in body, soul, and spirit. The virtues which go out from the presence of our Lord into our hearts are measured by our capacity to receive them; and that

---

[126] *Catech. Trid.* P. ii. c. iv. 2.
[127] Tobias xii. 21,22.
[128] Ps. xxxiii. 9.

capacity is measured by our preparation, both remote and proximate: that is, by our preparation before we go to the altar, and by our habitual union with God. Our Lord said: "In that day ye shall know that I am in the Father, and ye in Me, and I in you."[129] "In that day," that is, "when I am in the glory of the Father, and the Holy Ghost is come. Then you shall know that you are by substantial Communion of My Body and Blood in Me, and I in you." This consciousness of the Divine Presence dwelling within and encompassing us without is a mutual indwelling promised in these words. It was this that S. Paul meant when he said, "I live, yet not I, but Christ liveth in me." He becomes the Guide of all our living powers. They are elevated by union with Him, As every beat of the heart and every breath we draw is prevented and sustained by His creative power, so He prevents all our thoughts, words, and works. Our freedom and our agency are made perfect by union with Him. He is the presiding and Divine Agent who helps us in all things to do His will, but demands of us our whole personal obedience. We live, and act, and speak of our own freedom; but our freedom is guided and guarded by His grace and power. He lives in us, and we live by Him. What help can be wanting to a priest who loves his daily Mass? It contains all things — *Nutrit, praeservat, reparat, delectat et auget.* He is our food, our shelter, our refreshment, our delight, and our ever-growing strength.

2. The second help of a priest's life is the Divine Office. Seven times a day the acts of divine worship ascend from the Church throughout the

---

[129] S. John xiv. 20.

world to the throne of God. The Church in warfare, in suffering, and in heaven, adores the ever-blessed Trinity with an incessant voice of prayer and praise. The whole Church is the sanctuary, and the Divine Office is the ritual of the choir on earth uniting with the praises, thanksgivings, and doxologies which are the ritual of the choir in heaven. Every priest has his place in this choir, and he makes seven visits to the heavenly court day by day.

The Divine Office is a part of the divine tradition. It is a perpetual witness for God and for the faith. It has been wrought together by the hands of men; but those men were Saints, and their work was wrought under the guidance of the Holy Ghost. The framing of the ritual may have been the work of human hands; but the materials of which it is composed are the words of the Spirit of God. The Psalms and the Scriptures of inspired men under the Old Law and the New, with the writings of the Saints, are all interwoven into a wonderful texture of prayer and praise, of worship and witness of the kingdom of God, and of the Communion of Saints. The perpetual revolution of yearly solemnities and festivals — winter and spring, summer and autumn — brings round continually the whole revelation of faith. Prophets and Apostles, Evangelists and Saints, speak to us with voices that never die. The whole history of the kingdom of God is always returning upon our sight.

A devout soul asked of S. Peter Damian "why it is that we say *Dominus vobiscum*, as if many were present, when in truth none are there, and we are all alone?" He answered: "Because we are never alone. We are always worshipping with the whole

Church throughout the world, and we pray that the presence of the Lord may be with all the faithful upon earth." We say, "The Lord be with you," for we are adoring God on behalf of the whole visible Church, and in fellowship with those whose union with our Lord is already made perfect. We make these seven visits to the world of light and we recite the Holy Office because the Church lays it upon us under pain of mortal sin. We are bound to recite it for two reasons: the one, for the glory of God, the other, for our own sanctification. It is the wisdom and love of the Church for its priests that impose this grave obligation. The Church takes out of a priest's day so much of his time as his office requires, an hour and a half or two hours. That time no longer belongs to the priest, but to God and to the Church. The priest cannot alienate it, for it is not his own; but, under obedience and grave obligation, he is bound to use it for his own sanctification. The face of Moses shone after he had spoken with God; and our faces ought to shine, or our hearts at least ought to burn and to shine inwardly with the light of the heavenly court. When we say the hours, we "come to Mount Sion, and to the city of the living God, the heavenly Jerusalem, and to the company of many thousands of angels, and to the Church of the first born, who are written in the heavens, and to God the Judge of all, and to the spirits of the just made perfect."[130] What ought to be the habitual piety, recollection, humility in word and spirit, of one who, seven times a day, is in choir with the Saints, and before the face of God? Next to the Holy Mass, what greater help to sacerdotal perfection can there be than this?

---

[130] Heb. xii. 22,23.

3. A third help of the priest is mental prayer. The Divine Office is vocal prayer, but the mere recital of it fills the mind with the matter of mental prayer. A priest's life is the *vita mixta* of our Lord, and for our instruction Jesus spent days in toil and nights in prayer. A priest's life is both contemplative and active, and these two elements cannot be separated without loss and danger. *Haec meditare, in his esto, ut profectus tuus manifestus sit omnibus.* The things Timothy was to meditate and to live in were all the truths and precepts of the faith, but most especially "reading, exhortation, and doctrine" — that is, the deposit of the revelation in all its fulness and detail. In reading, our minds terminate upon a book; in meditation, our intelligence and our heart terminate upon God. Prayer is a vital act of faith and desire, to attain a fuller knowledge of God and a closer union with Him in affection and in resolution — that is, in heart and will.

The first effect of mental prayer is the realisation of the objects of faith — that is, of the world unseen as if it were visible, and of the future as if it were present. To realise is to have a vivid and abiding perception of things unseen as if they were palpable, and things future as if they were already come. We read of Moses that he endured the wrath of Pharao as seeing Him that was invisible. All the terror of the earthly king was lost in the sense of the Divine Presence behind the throne which overpowered all human majesty. S. Paul says we walk by faith, not by sight; but the objects of faith are eternal, the objects of sight are passing away. The invisible world is the substance, the visible world but the shadow. To minds that are not supernatural this world, loud and glaring, is palpable, and therefore thought to be real. The unseen is impalpable, and though not to be denied, yet upon such minds it has no action or constraining power. The great multitude of men live all day long as if there were no unseen world and no world to come. They do not meditate. They say prayers, but their prayers are not mental. The mind does not realise or aspire or stay itself upon God, upon the glory of the ever-blessed Trinity, upon the beauty of the sacred Manhood, upon the bliss of the Mother of God, upon the rest and joy of the Saints, upon the fellowship we have with them now, upon the share which is promised to us in their rest and joy hereafter, upon the presence of Jesus with us always, and the indwelling of the Holy Ghost in every pure and humble soul, above all in the soul of a pure and humble priest, of a faithful and fervent pastor. If we realise these things as the merchant realises the market place and his bales of merchandise, or the moneylender his securities and his coins of gold, then we shall live in this world, but not of it, as those who have risen with Christ[131] and are already "blessed with Him in heavenly places."[132] This realisation of unseen and heavenly things is better than all external rules to guard and strengthen a priest. It is an internal light and strength, which he carries with him at all times and in every place, sustaining the sacramental grace of his priesthood: and this is a divine and unfailing help in every peril or need.

4. Another potent help in a priest's life is preaching the Word of God to others. S. Paul said:

---

[131] Col. iii. 1.
[132] Ephes. i. 3.

"God sent me out not to baptise, but to preach the Gospel." The Council of Trent says that preaching is the chief office of Bishops;[133] and if it be the chief work of the Bishop, how much more of the priest. If Isaias was afraid to speak in the name of God because he was "a man of unclean lips"[134] what shall we judge of the sanctity and dignity of the preacher? If a prophet could hardly dare to preach in God's name, where shall the pulpit orators appear? That which was ordained for their help becomes unto them the occasion of falling. To be chosen out and to be sent by God to speak to men in His name, to come as a messenger *a latere Jesu* to preach penance and the remission of sins, to show the way of sanctity and of perfection in His name, in His words, and by His authority — who would dare these things if necessity were not laid upon him? To speak in God's name coldly, carelessly, and without due knowledge, without exact preparation, what rashness, what peril. To preach ostentatiously, with self-manifestation, vanity, and unreality[135] — how provoking to our Divine Master, how scandalous to souls. The simple, the humble, and the faithful instinctively detect the preacher who preaches himself; even men of the world, accustomed to the brief and peremptory language of earnest life, at once find out the unreal and the professional. They will listen to an honest preacher, though he be rude and rough.[136] The fewer of his own words and the

---

[133] Sess. xxiv. De Ref. c. iv.

[134] Isaias vi. 5.

[135] S. Augustine says of such: "Foris tumescit intus tabescit."

[136] S. Jerome says: "Multoque melius est a duobus imperfectis rusticitatem habere sanctam quam e!oquentiam peccatricem." — Ep. ad Nepot. tom. iv. p. 263.

more of God's words the surer he is to command the hearing and the respect of men. They feel that he has a right to speak, and that he is speaking in the name and in the words of his Master. They feel too that he has forgotten himself, and is thinking only of the message from God, and of the souls before him. He is teaching them what God has first taught him. He has prayed for it, and pondered on it; the truth has gone down through his intellect and his conscience into his own heart, and out of the fulness of it he speaks. The Wise Man says, "The mouth of the wise is in his heart; but the heart of the fool is in his mouth:" and a very shallow heart it is. If for "every idle word that men shall speak they shall give account in the day of judgment,"[137] what shall be the account of the words which we have spoken in long years and in a long life, as if in God's name? If the words of God by the prophet ought to be true of us as of himself, "Is not my word fire, and as the hammer that breaketh the rocks in pieces?" what shall be judged of our cold, light, interminable flow of words with few thoughts and empty rhetoric; idle because inefficacious, and inefficacious because our own? Whose heart have we set on fire? What hard heart have we broken? And if not, is it not because we have not first learned of God what we teach to others? If we sought it of Him He would give us a mouth and wisdom which even our adversaries would not be able to resist or to gainsay. The best meditation before preaching is prayer. We must, indeed, meditate what we preach, and make meditations in our sermons, but not sermons in our meditations; for our meditations are for our own sanctification, and we cannot more surely reach the

---

[137] S. Matt. xii. 36.

hearts of other men than by teaching what has first been realised in our own. For this reason the work of preaching the Word of God keeps us always as learners at the feet of our Divine Master. And in speaking His truth it reacts with a powerful effect upon ourselves. It deepens its outlines on our own intellect, conscience, and heart. It powerfully sustains our will; it replenishes our mind, keeping alive in our memory the meditations of long years that are past with continual fresh accessions of light. And it brings down a special blessing into the heart of the preacher. *Qui inebriat inebriabitur et ipse.* He that abundantly refreshes the souls of men with the water of life shall be abundantly refreshed himself. He that watereth shall be watered himself in the very time and act of speaking for God. A humble priest preaching as he prays is united with the fountain of the water of life; he has his lips to the spring: and he will often wonder at the thoughts which he never thought, and at the words which were put in his mouth. It is the promise, "He shall receive of Mine and show it unto you." *Ille plus dicit qui plus facit* — the few words of a holy priest do more than the many voices of human eloquence.

Preaching, then, is a constant and supernatural help to sacerdotal and pastoral perfection.

5. One more, and the last, we may enumerate is the confessional. S. Gregory the Great says that priests are like the laver of brass in the entrance of the Temple, in which the people took the water of purification before they entered. They receive the sins of all the people, but are kept always

pure themselves.[138] Jesus stretched out His hand and touched the leper, saying, "Be thou clean." The priest touches the sinner and is kept pure. But he needs to watch and pray, *ne lepra possit transire in medicum.*

We study moral theology in books, but there is no book so full of teaching as the confessional. The first time a priest sits in the tribunal of Penance can hardly be forgotten. On either side come alternate voices, as it were from heaven and from hell. First comes the confession of a sinner black as night; next the confession of a child in baptismal innocence; after that a penitent truly contrite, followed by a soul ignorant of itself and of its sinfulness; then come the poor, simple and single of heart; after them worldlings, intriguers, and evident liars. All the treatises of the Salmanticenses cannot teach a priest what his confessional is always teaching. If he has the humility to learn, it will teach him five great truths:

First, self-knowledge, by bringing things to his own remembrance, and by showing him his own face in a glass by the lives of sinners.

Secondly, contrition, in the sorrow of penitents who will not be consoled.

Thirdly, delicacy of conscience, in the innocent whose eye being single, and their whole body full of light, accuse themselves of omissions and deviations from the will of God, which we, perhaps, daily commit without discernment.

---

[138] *Reg. Pastoralis,* lit. ii. c. ii.

Fourthly, aspiration, by the fervent, whose one desire and effort, in the midst of burdened and restless homes, is to rise higher and higher in union with God.

Fifthly, self-accusation at our own unprofitableness, from the generosity and fidelity of those who are hindered on every side, and yet, in humility, self-denial, charity, and union with God, surpass us, who have every gift of time and grace needed for perfection.

But if we would learn these things, we must treat the Sacrament of Penance as we would treat the Sacrament of Baptism, realising its divine character and power. The first part of his duty that a lukewarm priest forsakes is the confessional. Sometimes he resents the rebukes which penitents unconsciously give. Sometimes he is weary of sitting long hours, and bearing with the rude and the repulsive. Sometimes he hears and absolves without a word because he has nothing to say, partly from a want of interior piety, and partly from not attending to the confession itself.

If, however, a priest rightly fulfils his office as father, judge, and physician, it becomes one of the most direct and powerful helps to his own sanctification.

What, then, can be wanting to sustain the priest in the perfection with which he was invested when he came for ordination? These five great sacerdotal graces, the Holy Mass, the Divine Office, the practice of mental prayer — that is, a life of contemplation — the preaching of the Word of God, the absolution of sinners, and the guidance of souls in the confessional, all react directly, powerfully, and profusely upon the life and mind of the priest. He can never plead for any fault of commission or of omission, or for yielding in any temptation, or for failure in any duty, that he had not the knowledge or the power to act up to his priesthood. Such a plea would be an accusation against our Divine Lord for commanding impossibilities, or exacting a hard service like an austere man, without providing adequate and abundant helps. It is a temptation, and a very common fault, to throw blame upon our state and circumstances, and to imagine that we should do better in some other state or way. If we fail under a full and fair trial with all helps around us, we should fail anywhere and in any condition and in any surroundings. If a priest's dangers are great, a priest's helps are greater.

CHAPTER IX.

THE PASTORAL OFFICE A SOURCE OF CONFIDENCE.

Beyond all doubt, the priest's helps are greater than the priest's clangers. But fear and anxiety can feel: they do not reason. The foresight of years of responsibility, the consciousness of our own weakness, the subtlety and strength of sin, the thought of our death-bed — all these weigh heavily at times upon us. The daily sight of sin; the wreck of many close around us, who began well and persevered long; the fall of priests who were our fellow-students and fellow-workers, or near friends; the memory how often we were near to the precipice, and our own feet had well-nigh slipped — these things keep alive a sense of fear in a priest's mind, and that fear is from the Holy Ghost. *Confige carnes meas timore tuo* ought to he our daily prayer. We have already seen many motives of confidence. We will dwell on one more and that is the pastoral office itself.

S. Peter three times denied his Master; three times Jesus asked him whether he loved Him; and three times He gave to Peter the pastoral care of His flock. This charge, therefore, was a sign of forgiveness, a proof of love, a pledge of salvation. This pledge was not exclusively given to Peter. It comes through Peter to us all. The pastoral care which we receive through him is to us also a test of our love, a proof of the love of Jesus, and a pledge of our salvation.

1. For first, to be a priest, as we have seen, is the highest predestination. The priest is called and ordained for the greatest glory of God. He is the first-fruits of the first-fruits of the new creation. He is called to the nearest approach to our Divine Redeemer, and to be a fellow-worker with Him in gathering out the elect from this evil world. In him are summed up all the tokens of acceptance that God ever gave to man. Peter of Blois says, "A priest has the primacy of Abel, the patriarchate of Abraham, the government of Noe, the order of Melchisedech, the dignity of Aaron, the authority of Moses, the perfection of Samuel, the power of Peter,

the unction of Christ."[139] These are all so many seals hanging to the writ of His promise to save us. They are not mere titles but realities. The Good Shepherd said of His disciples, "My sheep hear My voice; and I know them, and they follow Me. And I give them life everlasting; and they shall not perish for ever, and no man shall pluck them out of My hand. That which My Father hath given Me is greater than all, and no man can snatch them out of the hand of My Father,"[140] If we fall wilfully out of that divine hand we destroy ourselves. No power can pluck us out of it against our will, so long as our will and God's will are one. "If God had a mind to kill us, He would not have received a holocaust and libations at our hands, neither would He have shown us all these things, nor have told us the things that are to come."[141] Every token of acceptance in our work, every light and grace, our perseverance year after year, day after day, are pledges of our salvation. "I will not now call you servants, for the servant knoweth not what his lord doth. But I have called you friends, because all things whatsoever I have learned of the Father I have made known to you. You have not chosen Me, but I have chosen you, that you should go and should bring forth fruit."[142] To have been chosen by Him out of all the world is by itself a revelation of His purpose to save us. To call us out of His servants to be His friends: to admit us to the knowledge of His work and will: to make known also to us the communications of

---

[139] Serm. lx. ad Sacerdotes, Opp. p. 373.
[140] S. John X. 27-29.
[141] Judges xiii. 23.
[142] S. John XV. 15,16.

the Father: to have chosen us when we thought not of Him, to have made us capable of serving Him — each and all these signs of grace pledge to us that His will is steadfast to save us if we do not betray ourselves.

2. And next, to be a pastor is to possess the most abundant source of grace. We have already seen the unfailing supply of sacramental grace proportionate to our needs, duties, and dangers; and also the grace which attaches to the state in which we are. On this we need not dwell again; but there is a twofold discipline in the exercise of the pastoral office which aids us in a special degree in working out our salvation. The one is the continual augmentation of charity; the other is the continual exercise of self-denial.

"God is charity; and he that abideth in charity abideth in God, and God in him."[143] And God is the life of the soul. Where this life abides, except through our infidelity, the second death has no power. God will never revoke His gifts. He wills not the death even of a sinner. He pleads with him, "Why will ye die?"[144] "Ye will not come unto Me, that ye may have life."[145] He who loves God has the earnest and pledge of eternal life.

So S. Paul reasoned. His conversion, his call, his apostleship, his mission, were all pledges of the love of God, and of its immutability on God's part.

---

[143] 1 S. John iv. 16.
[144] Jer. xxvii. 13.
[145] S. John V. 40.

But our love to God may be increased all our life long. Every act of piety towards Him receives an augmentation of love. Every true prayer of the heart kindles the grace of charity. All mental acts of contemplation and adoration bring an increase of love into the soul of the least and the humblest, in the busiest and the most overburdened life. How much more in the life of a priest and of a pastor, whose whole toil in thought, word, and deed is in and for the kingdom of God. Every Mass we say, every recital of the Divine Office, may be an act springing from love to God, and drawing down accessions of love into the heart. The augmentation of charity in our union with God may go on accumulating every moment. Every aspiration, every desire, every inward act of obedience, patience, submission, and longing after God unites us more closely in love to Him, and enlarges our heart with His love, turning our hope into confidence, and quickening our course. *Viam mandatorum tuorum cucurri, cum dilatasti cor meum.*[146] As the heart is dilated the love of God increases, and as it increases it dilates the heart still more.

But where the love of God is, there is the love of our brethren. Where a fountain is, there is a stream. As a stream flows from a fountain, so the love of God pours itself out in love to man. The stream proves the fountain to be there. Therefore S. John says, "We know that we have passed from death unto life, because we love the brethren."[147] Our love to them proves our love to Him; and he that loves God abides in God, and has passed from

---

[146] Ps. cxviii. 32.
[147] 1 S. Jolin iii, 14.

death to life; for God is our eternal life, and He dwells in us even now. The continual exercise of brotherly love to all — to our flock, to our kindred, to our friends, and to our enemies — in all the extension of charity, is a discipline of perfection and of perseverance.

And this life of charity is more perfect in the proportion in which it exacts of us a mortification of self. But the sacerdotal or pastoral life is full of daily and hourly self-denial. We are called to die to ourselves, to our own wish and will and choice, and to be at the beck and bid of all, good and evil, reasonable and unreasonable, "becoming all things to all men, that I might save all."[148] It is a strange result of all our labour that only some may be saved. And yet for this we must die to ourselves, and go out of ourselves, and give up all right and claim over ourselves, for the elect's sake. The word *expropriatio* is full of a deep and searching sense. We "are not our own," we have lost all property in ourselves; for we are purchased by the most Precious Blood. This is S. Paul's meaning when he says, "We preach not ourselves, but Christ Jesus our Lord, and ourselves your servants through Jesus."[149] To be on our Master's side against sin, the world, and Satan, is not of our own act, but His who has predestinated and called us to His service. His will, and no will of ours, except under His preventing grace, has posted us in this warfare. "You have not chosen Me, but I have chosen you."[150]

---

[148] 1 Cor. ix. 22.
[149] 2 Cor. iv. 5.
[150] S. John xv. 16.

3. Lastly, to be set and sent to save others is either the lot of Judas or the lot of the beloved disciple. We may make it either. We may then well mistrust ourselves, and ask, "Lord, which am I?" But if we love the poor we need not doubt, for Judas cared not for the poor; and if we love our Divine Lord we cannot doubt, for Judas sold Him. We are not the beloved disciple, for he was sinless, and we are sinful; but we are disciples, and we are beloved, and our lot is full of the signs of salvation. S. Vincent of Paul said, "Jesus, why didst Thou come down upon earth? For the love of Thy neighhour. Poor priest, what has brought thee to this, to be cold and hungry and wearied, and all alone in the world, and in the wind and the weather and the winter? The love of souls." But who gave us this love? It is a sixth sense, which the few possess and the many cannot comprehend. The priest is called to show perfection in himself, and to exercise it upon others. He is not only saved to save others, but sanctified for their sanctification.[151] He is set as the light to give light, as the salt to resist corruption, as the good odour of Christ, like the censer between the living and the dead. If, after all this, he be a castaway, great indeed must be his infidelity to the Holy Ghost.

What motive to confidence is then wanting to the priest? He is encompassed by the signs of God's love and power. The will of God to save him

---

[151] "We must first be purified and theu purify others; be filled with wisdom and make others wise; become light and give light; be near to God and lead others to Him; be sanctified and sanctify; guide others by the hand and counsel them with knowledge."— S. Greg. Naz. Orat. ii. § lxxi.

eternally is made known to him by every token and pledge short of a direct and personal revelation. This strong and changeless confidence is a motive to self-oblation in greater things, and to self-denial in the less. Hope is a source of joy, and joy is a source of strength. The downcast and timid are weak and inert. The hopeful and confident are energetic and courageous. Fear does not honour our Divine Master. But trust springs from a perception of His love. Hope is a gift of the Holy Ghost, infused in Baptism and matured by exercise. S. Paul says that we are saved by hope, and he prays, "The God of hope fill you with all joy and peace in believing, that you may abound in hope and in the power of the Holy Ghost."[152]

Gedeon's three hundred men who lapped the water were of more worth in the battle than the multitude that drank kneeling, and the two-and-twenty thousands fearful and timorous who went away.[153] The proclamation sounds to this day along the whole line of those who aspire to the priesthood: "What man is there that is fearful and faint-hearted? Let him go and return to his house, lest he make the hearts of his brethren to fear, as he himself is possessed by fear."[154] When once posted by our Lord in the array of the battle no priest need fear. If he be faithful the hand of his Divine Master will be a helmet of salvation upon his head.

In all times of anxiety and fear and doubt and discouragement one may say: "God has

---

[152] Rom, XV. 13.
[153] Judges vii. 3-7.
[154] Deut. xx. 8.

foreknown and predestinated me to be a priest: He has called and justified and adopted me into the glory of His sons. He has sealed me with the mark of His soldiers and signed me with the character of His priests. He has guided and guarded me in youth and manhood, and has preserved me to this day, supporting my perseverance by the ever-present and unfailing help of His manifold grace in every time of need. In every change of the warfare which is against me, I know that He wills my salvation. What has He left undone that He could do to save me? One thing He will never do: He will never take away from me my free will. And this is my only danger. If I freely betray myself or forsake Him, then I shall perish; but if my will is united with Him, He will guide and guard me, not only from my enemies without, but even from myself. If only I have no will to grieve Him, and a true will to hold fast by Him, He will keep me even unto death." 'The sure foundation of God standeth firm, having this seal. The Lord knoweth who are His, and let every one depart from iniquity who nameth the name of the Lord.'"[155]

Our very state, then, is the highest ground of confidence.

The state and work of priests and of pastors, if we are faithful to our Divine Master, is blessed everywhere throughout the universal Church. In the countries of the Old World, where the world is strong and corrupt, and faith and piety are weak, they who have the cure of souls have much to suffer. To watch a flickering and departing life is the

---

[155] 2 S. Tim. ii. 19.

saddest office of love and patience. The nations and people of the Old World for three hundred years have been descending, some rapidly and with violence, some slowly and insensibly but steadily, from the light and order of faith. Spurious reformation has generated revolution, and revolution has desecrated the sovereignties and states of Christendom, leaving the Church isolated as in the beginning. The pastors of the flock have many sorrows over souls that are rushing to perdition, and for the outrages wreaked upon the Church. It is a grievous thing to see a Catholic or a Christian people turning its back to the light. Nevertheless, faithful pastors have the peace of knowing that they are on God's side, and that they are contending for the rights of God. In all their sorrows there is this deep joy, which none can take from them. S. John Chrysostom says: "The warfare of monks is great, and their labours many; but if one compare their toils to a priesthood, well discharged, he will find as great a difference as between a private man and a king."[156] And their consolation is in like proportion.

But if this be true in the older regions of the Church, how much more is it true in England. Among us the Church is both old and new. We are a handful, but separate from the world, and from courts, and from the corrupt atmosphere of secular patronage and secular protection. The true protection of the Church is its own independence, and its true power is its own liberty. We are pastors of a flock descended from martyrs and confessors, and their fervour is not extinct in their posterity. We

---

[156] *De Sacerdotio*, lib. vi. 5

are in a special sense pastors of the poor; for the rich have gone away, and the vast prosperity of England is in hands that know us not. But to live among the poor was the lot of our Divine Master, and to share His lot is a pledge of His care. We are not only pastors of the poor, but poor ourselves. Poverty is the state of the priesthood in this the richest of all the kingdoms of the world. We are here bound together in mutual charity and service. Our people are united to us in a generous love and mutual trust; and our priests are united to each other and to their Bishops. They are united to each other with bonds of fraternal love as close as, if not closer than, can be found in any region of the Catholic unity. If all these things be for us, what shall be against us?

CHAPTER X.

THE VALUE OF A PRIEST'S TIME.

Next to grace time is the most precious gift of God. Yet how much of both we waste. "We say that time does many things. It teaches us many lessons, weans us from many follies, strengthens us in good resolves, and heals many wounds. And yet it does none of these things. Time does nothing. But time is the condition of all these things which God does in time. Time is full of eternity. As we use it so we shall be. Every day has its opportunities, every hour its offer of grace. The Council of Sens applies the words, "Behold, I stand at the door and knock," to the continuous action of the Holy Ghost upon the heart. This is true of every living soul. The faithful have all through life and all the day long this constant invitation and aid to lay up for themselves a greater reward in eternity. As a man soweth so shall he also reap, both in quantity and in kind. All men have their seed-time and their harvest in time and for eternity. If we lose the seed-time we lose the harvest. Another seed-time and another harvest may he granted to us. But it is another. That which is lost is lost for ever.

Now if time he so precious to all, is it not most precious above all to a priest? And happy is he who can give account of his time. Some men seem to have no knowledge of its value. Some never think of it. Some are so inert that it runs away before they stir to use it. Some are so indolent that they consciously waste it. Some are so irregular and unpunctual that time wastes itself. They are always in a hurry, always late, never ready, never prepared.

There are two questions in Holy Writ which a priest will do well to remember wheresoever he goes. The one is the question of God to Elias when on Mount Horeb he was mourning- without moving: *Quid hic agis, Elia?* — "What dost thou here, Elias?" This question would keep us away altogether from many places, and would hasten our leaving many more. The other question is our Lord's: "Did you not know that I must be about My Father's business?" This we may well bear in mind when kind and hospitable friends invite us to be with them, or when our own infirmity makes us turn to recreation or to human sympathy, or even to work lying out of the furrow in which we are, each one, set to guide the plough. Who can measure the value of a priest's time? If the time of all men is full of eternity, the time of a priest is full not of his own eternity only, but of the eternity of multitudes both known and unknown to him. We will try, then, to measure its value.

1. The first measure of the value of our time is the Holy Mass. The first-fruits of a priest's time belong to God, and they are offered every morning in the Holy Mass. Half an hour of preparation and half an hour of thanksgiving ought never to be given up to any other use or purpose, for they are not ours to give away. This is the first measure of the value of our time. In it we speak with God, commune with our Divine Master, and give thanks to the ever-blessed Trinity. What should be the fervent use of the hours of a day that is so begun? The fragrance and the fervour of it ought to be upon us all day long, pervading it with a sense of our relation to our Master in heaven, and teaching us to be as avaricious of time, as impatient of its loss, and as watchful in guarding it from being stolen from us as the world is of its money. God so values time that He gives it to us only day-by-day, hour-by-hour, moment-by-moment. And He never gives us a moment without taking the last away. We have never two hours or two moments at once. Every moment in the day we may, if we will, renew the intention with which we said Mass in the morning. We may revive our prayers and thanksgivings at least by an aspiration. Our whole day would then be virtually pervaded by our Mass and Communion.

2. A second measure of value is the knowledge a priest may lay up by a punctual use of his time. *Labia sacerdotis custodient scientiam.* But how shall the lips of the priest keep the science of God

and of souls unless he be a man of sacred study? The theology of our early days is soon obscured by the failure of memory, and by the dust of a busy life. And therefore how precious is every moment a priest can redeem from active work to return to his old books, or to go further and deeper into his earlier studies. It is a good thing to have certain books always open, to be read at any moment that can be seized. There ought to be even in the busiest life certain *horae subsecivae*. We call them vaguely leisure hours. They are the hours that are cut out, as it were, by stealth from the main duties and works of the day. No better test than this can be found to see whether a priest knows the value of his time. Some men do everything as if they did nothing; and some men do nothing as if they did everything. A priest who values his time seldom fails to find enough for everything. A punctual mind can so order the hours of the day as to take out of them, and to use the intervals between successive works and duties. Some books of close and continuous matter need an hour of quiet attention; some of a less precise kind may he read in times caught flying; and some may he taken up at any moment. A hard student once advised a friend to have "five-minute books." And many a book could be read through in a year by five minutes a day. All that is needed is the habit of attention, and a firm will not to leave what we read till we understand it, be it only a page, or no more than a sentence. Perhaps some one will say that this is taxing a priest's time too severely. But if we will ask ourselves how much time in the day is given to books that are not necessary, to newspapers, to prolonged conversation, to visits which are not either pastoral or beneficial, to lingering, and doubting what to read and what to do — if we were to cast up all this, the most fervent would find that much time has been stolen from him, much has been wasted, not a little misapplied.

3. A third measure of the value of our time is what we might do in it, if spent in the confessional. There is no surer sign of a fervent priest than the love of the confessional. It is the first duty that a lax priest avoids and evades. To sit for long hours day-by-day and night-by-night, without impatience and without loss of temper, is a sure sign of the love of souls. We need not attempt to measure the comparative value of preaching and of hearing confessions. They are incommensurable. Each has its own proper character. But many have a great zeal and promptness to preach who are slow and tardy to sit in the confessional. There is no manifestation of self, no natural excitement, no subtle allurements of a personal kind in sitting for long hours listening to the sins, and sorrows, and often the inconsiderate talk of multitudes, for the most part unknown. It is like fishing with a single line. Long hours of waiting are rewarded by one solitary gain. But it is, in the highest sense of the word, the pastor's work — that is, the care of souls. And it demands in a high degree an abnegation of self, a repression of personal infirmities of temper, and a generous love of souls, especially of the poor.

But what use of time can be compared to this care and guidance of souls?[157] Knowing that we

---

[157] "For indeed this seems to me to be the art of arts and the science of sciences, to direct men, the most manifold and most variable of animals." — S. Greg. Naz. Orat. ii. xvii. tom. i. p. 21.

have the power of binding and loosing, and that in the confessional souls that are perishing are brought to penance, and the penitent are led onward to perfection; that the innocent are guarded in their union with God, and that God is glorified both in them that are saved and in them that perish, it would seem to be the first instinct of a priest to give to the confessional as many days and as many hours as he can. Instead of finding it a weariness, it would be his consolation. Instead of shortening the hours or lessening the number of his days for confession in the church, he would extend them if possible, and encourage his brethren in the cure of souls to do likewise.

But it is not only in church that the patience and charity of a confessor are tested. All that has been said applies especially to the care of the sick, and to the willingness we ought to have to give time to instruct, to console, and to encourage them, above all when death is near. The sick and the dying can hardly think for themselves. The burden of a suffering or dying body dulls and deadens the mind. It is in that time of sorrow and fear that the voice of a true pastor cheers and supports the helpless. His words and whispers of faith and hope, and contrition and confidence, with the promises of God, and the holy names of Jesus, Mary, and Joseph, fill the mind that can no longer think for itself with light, and peace, and consolation. It is not enough to administer mechanically the last Sacraments. There are needed also the last consolations and the last compassion of the Good Shepherd, who knows His sheep and is known by them as their help and solace in the last passage to eternity.

4. Another measure of the value of our time is what may be done in it by prayer. When S. Paul said "Pray without ceasing," [158] he did not use rhetorical exaggeration. He meant that we may be always and everywhere speaking with God, by our aspirations, desires, and will. They who live in union with God, conscious of His presence, and referring all their life to Him, not only pray when they speak with God, but when they work for Him. *Laborare est orare*. A pastor's whole life may be a life of communion with Him. The value of time spent in prayer may be measured in two ways: first, in the answers it receives; and next, in its reaction upon ourselves. As to the answers, who can say what they lose who pray little, and what they gain who habitually speak with God? The work of priests and pastors is so expressly supernatural that we look for supernatural results, and we ask them as such from God. The conversion of sinners and the salvation of souls virtually contain all the works of our spiritual ministry, and they are so distinctly divine in their origin and supernatural in their instruments that we ask them as gifts, not as results of our own agency. There can be little doubt that the fertility of the lives of some pastors and the barrenness of others depend upon, and are measured by, their prayers. They who pray most will receive most; they who pray little will receive less. But of all this I need not speak. There is nothing we may not ask, either absolutely or conditionally; and there is nothing good that He will not give us: for to pour out His gifts upon us is His bliss. But it is the reaction of prayer upon ourselves that gives us a prompt and certain

---

[158] 1 Thess. V. 17.

measure. We are what we are before God, and nothing else, neither better nor worse. And we are what our communion with God makes us. Our faces shine, or are dim or darkened, as we are nearer or farther from God in prayer. A calm, recollected, joyous, hopeful mind is the reward of prayer. A restless, wandering, sad, and timid mind is the consequence of not praying as we ought. In truth, prayer measures our state; and what we are our work will be. A priest who prays much will do in an hour what a priest who prays less will hardly do in many days. The words of a priest always united with God have a life, a warmth, an energy, and a persuasion which no natural gifts can give. We do little because we pray little; and because we pray little we are what we are. If the time we lose, if the hours that are stolen from us, were spent in speaking with God instead of with the world, all we do would be higher in spirit, deeper in results, and more lasting in its effect.

5. A last measure of the value of a priest's time is in the end for which he exists.

He is to be a witness for his Divine Master in teaching and testifying to the truth; but chiefly by the visible example of his life, and by the conscious and unconscious influence of his mind. Woe to him if he be found a false witness in the least of the commandments of God, or in the influence of his mind and life. And great is the peril and unfaithfulness if he be an ambiguous, or equivocal, or obscure witness. He would be like a warning by the wayside which no man can read. And for those who perish by his fault he will be held to answer.

He is also to be a light in the world. But if his mind and life show only a dim or unsteady light, who will trust his guidance?

He is also to be the salt that purifies the mind, and the life and the society of other men. But if he be not pure in deed, word, or thought, contact with him will rather harm than help those that are about him. His influence is never negative. He is always giving or taking away, gaining or losing for himself and for others.

How great is the danger of a priest living and labouring in the world all men can see. His field of work is the world, in the midst of the wheat and the tares. The evil-minded are often less dangerous, for they are open enemies: but the good, who are often unwise, or light, or lukewarm, throw him off his guard by their goodness, and lower him before he is aware. They waste his time by their visits: they devour it by their invitations: they entangle him by their talk: they encompass him by what is called society — that is, by people of all kinds, and by recreations which, though without sin, are out of all proportion and out of all harmony with the gravity of the priesthood. Intimacies easily and unconsciously at first spring up; fascinations and personal attractions disturb the calm of his mind: and the equilibrium of his spiritual life is lost. The conversation and the presence of some one becomes so alluring as to be a part of his thoughts, and a daily need. A false relation is insensibly formed, free perhaps from all sin, but full of an unbalanced attachment, which draws him from our Divine Master, the priest's only Friend, to whom his whole heart was given. What nets for his feet lie in his path, what pits are open in his way. How insensibly he goes onward, not measuring the distance, till a gulf opens behind him, and his past is almost out of sight. All this is also a measure of time: not that time has done it. But he has done it in time, and in the time he has wasted and given away, or the time that has been stolen from him.

Against this the truest and surest remedy is a wise and resolute use of our days and hours. No man ought to be without a twofold *Horarium*. The first part is for his day: fixing the hour of rising and of going to rest, of Mass and office, of study and writing, of the work of souls in the confessional, and in the homes of the sick and of the poor. And such a *Horarium* ought to fix the measure and quantity of time allotted to each of these divisions of the day. There is here no head left for the world or for society, for a priest's life is out of the world; his home and his Divine Friend are in the sanctuary; the Saints, and the teachers who speak to him through his books, are his society. When the sun is down, the evening is the most precious part of a priest's day.

It is the only time he can call his own. Happy the priest who knows its value, and unwise the priest who wastes it in the world.

The other part of the *Horarium* is for a calculation of the way in which our life speeds away. Most men give one-third of every day to sleep, with its circumstances of rising and lying down: about three hours are due to Mass and office: who can say how much to private prayers and spiritual reading, to study, to the confessional, to the care of souls?

and of all this who can fix the measure? To the world and to society some priests give little; many give too much. If, then, we live to seventy years, we shall have spent more than three-and-twenty years in sleep: about seven years in Mass and offices — that makes up about thirty out of seventy years. How are the other forty years bestowed? It would be well for us if in every place we heard the words, *Quid hic agis, Elia?*[159] and in every hour of our day, "Did you not know that I must be about My Father's business ?"

CHAPTER XI.

THE PRIEST'S SORROWS.

We read twice in the Gospels that Jesus wept, and only once that He "rejoiced in the Holy Ghost."[160] He wept at the grave of Lazarus, and over Jerusalem when He saw it from the Mount of Olives. He rejoiced when He gave thanks to His Father because the mysteries of His kingdom were revealed, not to the wise of this world, but to the humble and childlike. Our Lord was the Man of Sorrows; and a priest must in this too be like Him, for the disciple is not above his master. But the three-and-thirty years of mental sorrow did not make our Divine Lord morose or melancholy or of a clouded countenance. The fruit of the Spirit was in Him in all fulness, and "the fruit of the Spirit is

---

[159] 3 Kings xix. 9,13.
[160] S. Luke x. 21.

charity, joy, peace."[161] No countenance was ever more radiant with a divine love and joy than His. And we shall not be like our Master if our countenances are sad and our voices mournful. Nevertheless, a priest must be a man of sorrows. If he has the intuition of faith to see the sin of the world, and a heart of compassion to feel for the havoc of death both in body and soul, he must share in the sorrows of our Divine Redeemer.

1. The first sorrow of a priest is the consciousness of his own unworthiness.

The words of S. Paul must be in the mind of every priest: "I give Him thanks who hath strengthened me, even to Christ Jesus our Lord, for that He hath counted me faithful, putting me in the ministry, who before was a blasphemer and a persecutor and contumelious. But I obtained the mercy of God because I did it ignorantly in unbelief. New the grace of our Lord hath abounded exceedingly with faith and love, which is in Christ Jesus. A faithful saying, and worthy of all acceptation, that Christ Jesus came into this world to save sinners, of whom I am the chief. But for this cause have I obtained mercy, that in me first Christ Jesus might show forth all patience for the information of them that shall believe in Him unto life everlasting"[162] These words show that S. Paul did not count himself to be faithful; that he was conscious of his great past unworthiness; that he was forgiven because he sinned in ignorance; that he knew no one more sinful than himself; and that for

---

[161] Gal. v. 22.
[162] 1 S. Tim. i.12-16.

this very cause he was chosen, that he might be a living witness of the patience of Jesus and an evidence of the sovereign grace of salvation, that none should ever despair.

What priest can look back without wondering that he should have been called to be a priest? How many of our early companions were every way more fit than we. They never committed a multitude of sins, follies, imprudences, we know of ourselves. Much we did knowing well that we ought not to do it; much we see now in a light which we then, through our own fault, had not. Of no one do we know so much evil as we know of ourselves; not perhaps of literal breaches of the law, but of great spiritual sins in the midst of great spiritual graces. The love, forgiveness, hope, confidence, and salvation we preach to others is to be seen first in ourselves. If His mercy had not been infinite, we should not only not be priests, but we should not even exist.

"What man knoweth the things of a man save the spirit of a man that is in him?"[163] They that know most of us know little of the world of inward life reaching back to our earliest consciousness. Our whole life is suspended in it as if now present in one view — childhood, boyhood, youth, manhood, distinct but continuous, seen all in one moment; there are lights of great brightness descending from God, and spots very dark blotting the light ascending from ourselves. How is it possible that I should be chosen to be a priest? I know more sins of my own than of my companions in boyhood who

---

[163] 1 Cor. ii. 11.

were not called to come so near to God. Was it that He saw that I should not otherwise be saved? that I am not fit to battle with the world, or even to live in the world? that without the surroundings and supports of a priest's life and state I should have sunk under the fraud, or force, or fascinations of the world? When I remember what I was, how can I dare to take the word of God in my mouth? When I warn men against sin, why do they not say, "Physician, heal thyself"? When I tell them of their faults, I hear them say, "Thou hast a beam in thine own eye," and, as S. Gregory says, *ulcus in facie*. And when I preach the reign of the love of God in the heart, and generosity, and self-oblation, knowing what I am — my impatience yesterday and my shrinking to-day — a voice says to me, "Thou whited wall." Every priest who knows himself will know what it is to be discouraged, saddened, depressed by a multitude of crosses and disappointments, but none are so heavy to bear as our own conscious unworthiness. S. Gregory of Nazianzum says of himself: "This held me in a lower state, and made me humble, that it was better to hear *'the voice of praise'* than to profess myself a teacher of things beyond my powers; namely, the majesty, the sublimity, the greatness (of God), and the pure natures which hardly apprehend the splendour of God, whom the abyss hides, whose hiding-place is the darkness, being the purest light, and inaccessible to the multitude, who is in all and out of all; who is all beauty and above all beauty; who illuminates and eludes the speed and the sublimity of the mind, always withdrawing in the measure in which He is apprehended, and raising him who loves Him upwards by fleeing from him, and when held passing from his hands."[164]

Who has not remembered the day of his ordination, and said, "who will grant me that I might be according to the months past, according to the day in which God kept me? When His lamp shined over my head, and I walked by His light in darkness. As I was in the days of my youth, when God was secretly in my tabernacle."[165]

2. Another sorrow of a priest arises from the sins of his bad people. The chief and lifelong mental sorrow of Jesus came from the daily contact of His divine sanctity with the sin of the world. Looking upon the distortion and defacement of the creation of God, He said, "O just Father, the world hath not known Thee." The world knows not its Maker. It is a profound contempt of the Divine Majesty not to know Him. And yet for those that knew not what they did Jesus prayed upon the Cross. But who is there in our charge that does not know God? Even the grossest ignorance is an affected ignorance. If we have in us the heart of our Master, the sins on every side of us, sins of the flesh and of the spirit, the havoc and ravage of Satan in men, women, children, must be a ceaseless sorrow. In the measure in which we have a hatred of sin and a love of souls, the spiritual death of our people will be always a perceptible and personal grief. Ill-usage and ingratitude can be borne patiently. All that men can say or do against us is of little weight. A priest is *signum cui contradicetur*: he is a butt for all the slings

---

[164] Orat. ii. § lxxvi. tom. i. p. 49.
[165] Job xxix. 2-4.

and stones of false and evil tongues; but though this can do us no hurt, yet to be hated, scorned, and ridiculed is cutting to flesh and blood. Nevertheless, this brings little sorrow. It may excite resentment, but resentment dries up sorrow. Sorrow comes from love, compassion, pity for souls: such a sorrow is a sign of likeness to the Good Shepherd. As S. Paul said to the Corinthians who turned against him, "I most gladly will spend, and he spent myself, for your souls, although loving you more, I be loved less."[166] Our Lord also had said before: "If the world hate you, you know that it hated Me before it hated you."[167] To be hated, therefore, is a countersign of our fidelity.

"We live with the vision of souls that are dead continually before our eyes. The plain of the dry bones was spectral, but the revelry and surfeiting of souls that are spiritually dead is far more ghastly. But it needs a spiritual intuition to discern it: therefore some men can live in the midst of it without perceiving it; and even we, who ought to have the first-fruits of the Spirit, perceive it only in the measure of our discernment.

Men of evil life are murderers of souls. By direct intention, or by the infection of example, they destroy the innocent and turn back the penitent. We can see the plague spreading from home to home, from soul to soul. The reign of sin and the shadow of death settle upon souls and homes over which we have long been watching, but in vain. Sometimes Satan seems all but visible: his presence palpable,

---

[166] 2 Cor. xii. 15
[167] S. John xv. 18.

and his power may be felt in the overthrow of years of labour. In every flock there will be the enemies of God, open and declared, clandestine and concealed. Of all such S. Paul says: "Of whom I have told you often, and now tell you weeping, that they are enemies of the Cross of Christ, whose end is destruction, whose god is their belly, whose glory is in their shame, who mind earthly things."[168]

3. But besides the sins of bad men, a priest has to suffer by the lukewarmness of good men. That people should be so good, and yet not better; that they should be so full of light, and yet fall so short of it; that they should do so many good acts, and yet not do more; that they should have so few faults, but so few excellences; that they should be so blameless, but deserve so little praise; so full of good feeling, but so spare in good works; so ready to give, but so narrow in their gifts: so regular in devotions, yet so little devout; so pious, yet so worldly; so ready to praise the good works of others, and yet so hard to move to do the like; so full of censures of the inertness and inconsistency, omissions, faults, and lukewarmness of other men, and yet so unhelpful and soft and unenergetic and lukewarm themselves — all these are spiritual paradoxes and contradictions which vex and harass a priest with perpetual disappointment. Where he looked for help he finds none; where he thought he could trust he finds his confidence betrayed; where he thought to lean for support he finds the earth give way. There is something in sorrow for sin which unites us with God. It alarms, and warns us that we are in the front of the battle, and that we can never put off the

---

[168] Philip, iii. 18,19.

"whole armour of God." It is a wrestling with spiritual wickedness in the high places of subtlety and strength, in which souls perish before our eyes, and we ourselves are in danger. This braces and confirms our courage and self-command. But the petty and paltry faults of good people, the littleness and the selfishness, the self-pleasing and the refined insensibility to the sorrows, sufferings, and sins that are around them — these things irritate and provoke without rousing our self-control. "We are tempted to fret and complain under our disappointments from good people; and we understand S. Paul's disappointment when he said, "I have no man so of the same mind, who with sincere affection is solicitous for you; for all seek the things that are their own, not the things that are Jesus Christ's."[169] As a rule, they who talk most do least, and they who are always asking why this or that is not done are the last to do what is needed. Our people may be divided into talkers and doers: the doers are silent, and the work is done; the talkers mostly find fault with the way of doing it, and the work itself when done. Complaining is their contribution to the work, and they give little else. It is sad and strange how few will give their personal service. They will give money, but not time and trouble. Almsgiving has less self-denial than personal work. But personal care of the sick or the sorrowful or the sinful is more precious in God's sight than all gold and silver.

  4. Another of the sorrows of a priest is from false brethren. Under this name may be classed not only apostates and men of unsound faith, but

---

[169] Philip, ii. 20,21.

dissemblers and betrayers of secrets, and whisperers and murmurers and detractors, and those who hang about a priest's house, and note and observe and pick up and carry away every discontent and grief and grudge that is against him. Such men are usually profuse in words of respect and of personal attachment and of devoted loyalty. Their reverence is servile, and their professions of goodwill beyond all measure. Who can suspect such men without rash judgment and an ungenerous mind? The better a priest is, the more trustful he will be. He believes others to be as himself; he hates dissimulation, and believes other men to be incapable of it. Therefore he answers simply and without suspicion, and where he can speak out he tells the questioner all he wants to know. In a little while a cloud of misunderstandings, misrepresentations, and misstatements come like gnats about the priest's head. Whence, why, and what about, who can tell? Friendships are broken, resentments are kindled, the parish is divided, dissensions separate families. At last the poor priest remembers the day and the man and the questions. It is a lesson for life; not the first, perhaps, nor the last. And yet people blame him for reserve and silence, as if it had not been burnt into him by cautery. False brethren are bad enough; but false sisters are worse, in the measure in which they are less accurate in hearing and more unwearied in retailing.

These things are vexatious; but there are worse still. There are false brethren who carp at every act of authority, and criticise every word. They are thoroughly out of harmony with those who are over them. The parish priest never does right, and can do nothing aright. And this murmuring infects others with discontent. These things, in themselves contemptible, will nevertheless set a parish in contention against their priest. A spirit of criticism, once roused, is ravenous and unrelenting. Peace and charity are destroyed, and ill-will arises between flock and pastor, from whose hands they receive the absolution of the most Precious Blood and the Bread of eternal life. At first sight some may wonder why S. Paul, after summing up a black list of the sins of the flesh, adds "enmities, contentions, emulations, wraths, quarrels, dissensions, sects," and closes the list with "murders, drunkenness, revellings, and suchlike."[170] In truth, the spiritual sins of "enmities and dissensions" are more Satanic than the sins of the flesh, for Satan has no body; and they are more at variance with God, because they are spiritual, and God is charity.

5. The last great sorrow of a priest that can now be added is the fall of a brother priest. It may be of one who has grown up with him from boyhood, and was ordained with him on the same day, or of one over whom he has watched with the care and hope of an elder brother. He was once innocent, bright in mind, single of heart, his intelligence full of light, and his natural powers largely unfolded. His outset was full of promise. Every one looked forward to a life of multiplying usefulness and of sacerdotal perfection. All at once, as a tree breaks asunder and shows decay at the heart, he falls, or little by little the leaves grow pale and droop, and a sickliness which none can understand overspreads the tree. Some secret temptation, some perilous allurement, some

---

[170] Gal V, 10 21.

unchastened intimacy, some clouding of the conscience, some relaxation of rule, some neglect of self-examination, some omissions of prayer, some fatal opportunity, when conscience is silenced, and the will is weak and the temptation strong — then comes the first fall, after which to fall again and again is easy. The gulf is passed, and he enters upon an unknown world *ubi nullus ordo et umbra mortis*. He wonders to find himself in a state so strange and new, and to be so little afraid. Once he thought that after such a fall he should have died; but now he finds his life whole in him. And God only, and one more, know the truth, and the truth need never come out. The seal of confession will cover it; and outwardly he is the same man — priest and pastor. Who shall know it if he do not betray himself? To shrink from work, to cease to be seen and heard, would call attention and awaken curiosity. He goes on as before, or rather he is more seen and more heard than ever. Nobody suspects him. The stone in the wall is silent, and the timber in the roof does not cry out; who, then, can know? Nobody could prove anything, even if people suspect. Safety is impunity, and impunity leads to impenitence. In the end all comes out into the light, not so much by the search of man as by the finger of God. Long impunity gives time and occasion for a long career of reiterated sins, and a daily practice of simulating piety and of dissembling sin hardens his forehead and his heart. He defies all witnesses, denies all evidence, and persists in deceiving all who can be deceived. But the priest who loves him, and knows all, cannot be deceived; and his sorrow is for the soul on which the sacerdotal character was indelibly impressed in the day when he was consecrated to be the light of the world, the salt of the earth, the image of the Son of

God, a shepherd of the sheep. His sorrow is also for the souls that have been wrecked by the priest in his fall; for the scandal to the faithful and to those that are without, and for the sanctity of the priesthood which has been stained, and for the Church which has been dishonoured, and for our Divine Master, who has been once more sold and betrayed. What sorrow can go beyond this? All that can be said is, "Alas, alas, my brother!"[171]

---

[171] 3 Kings xiii. 30.

CHAPTER XII.

THE PRIEST UNDER FALSE ACCUSATIONS.

God might have redeemed the world by a manifestation of His glory; but He chose to do it by shame. Jesus was rejected of men, and they hid their faces from Him as if ashamed to own Him. This lot He has bequeathed to us. Jesus was falsely accused. No man ever more so. He was called a Samaritan, and told that He had a devil. He was "a gluttonous man and a wine-bibber, a friend of publicans and sinners." He was a deceiver, and a seducer, and seditious; stirring up the people, feigning to be a king and a prophet, being a pretender and a blasphemer. He suffered all the penalties of sin, its guilt only excepted.

1. False accusation was hateful to Him, because of His perfect holiness. To be baptised as if He were a sinner was an act of divine humility. The eyes of all were fixed upon Him. He was counted as one of the sinners of Jerusalem. It was bitter to be even suspected. But to be accused as a sinner was an infinite humiliation. The bitterness of sin entered into His sinless soul. He tasted the horror and the shame even of those who are justly accused. Innocent men arraigned at the bar, and though falsely yet skilfully accused of atrocious crimes, have afterwards told us that, for a time, they had the horrible sense of guilt upon them. And, in the measure of their innocence, their hatred of the evil laid to their charge will be more acute. To the sinful it brings little pain; for sin deadens the perception of the baseness, the grossness, the deadliness of sin.

The agony of our Divine Lord in the Garden came from the vision and the contact of the sin of the world. The sins of mankind before the Flood, the sins of the tribes of Israel, the sins of the Christian world, and, above all, the sins of His own priests — these wrung from Him a sweat of blood. The sanctity of God in contact with the sin of the world caused a sorrow "unto death." For though God cannot sorrow as God, God Incarnate sorrowed by the suffering of His sinless humanity in this world of sin.

In the measure, then, of the innocence and purity of a priest's life and heart will be his suffering when falsely accused. They who accuse him little know the pain they inflict. They have not his delicacy of conscience, or the purity of his heart, or his jealousy for the priesthood and for the Name of our Divine Master. So far "they know not what they do." The coarse, and the rude, and the vindictive, and the malevolent, and even the foolish and the reckless in speech, with no ill will, perhaps, but with great want of caution, often inflict wounds upon a good priest which are never healed. They would care little if it were said of themselves; and that is, perhaps, their only excuse, and a very mean one.

2. And the false accusations against our Divine Saviour came from those to whom He was always doing good. For three long years in meekness and gentleness He spoke with them of the kingdom of God. He healed their sick, and cleansed their lepers, and opened the eyes of their blind, and fed the hungry, and raised their dead. And the people heard Him gladly, and the little children came to Him without fear. Virtue went out of Him to

illuminate, to sanctify, and to console. And yet He was hated; and at one time they sought to kill Him, at another to cast Him down from the hill on which they dwelt. And they spoke against Him, and accused Him falsely. They returned hatred for His love, and reviling for His patience. This added a special pain.

Every priest must be ready to bear the same. Those for whom we have done most are often the most thankless; and at the first reproof or the first refusal, however small, break out into bitter ill-will. It is a proverb that men forget the score of times that we have said yes, and remember only the once that we say no. Of the ten lepers only one returned to give thanks, and he was a Samaritan. Priests, Levites, and Jews passed the wounded man by the wayside. Only one was found to help him, and he, too, was a Samaritan. The Jews were blinded with the excess of light, and surfeited with the abundance of their mercies. They took all as a right, and crucified the Lord of glory. But the Samaritans, in their austere scarcity of light and grace, were quicker to perceive the goodness and the law of God. So it is often in our flock. The favoured become pampered, and they who have had least care have most gratitude.

3. And the false accusations came especially from those who knew Him. We read that at one time even His brethren did not believe in Him. And at last one of His twelve disciples betrayed Him. It often happens that a priest is falsely accused by some one for whom he has had a special intimacy, and on whom he has bestowed a special care. It may be some soul ready to perish whom he has

plucked as a brand from the burning. It often happens that they for whom we do most are least grateful and most malicious. Because so much has been done for them, they exact more; and because more cannot be done, they break out in jealousy and vindictiveness. It would be but a little thing if enemies who do not know us speak against us; but when familiar friends, who have been freely admitted to our confidence and within our guard, who have lived under our roof and broken bread with us — when they turn and accuse us, it is far more bitter. *Inimici hominis domestici ejus.* The care and kindness and forbearance we have shown to them is all lost. Some passion of jealousy or self-interest has mastered them. They first turn from us, and then turn upon us. If they had been strangers and unknown, we could have better borne it; but from them it has a manifold ingratitude. They know us better than other men. Their accusations are not from ignorance or mistake. They know the falseness, because they know the truth: and that galls them. They can find nothing against us truly; therefore they are irritated, and go to Satan's forge for lies. Sister Emmerich says that Satan in Gethsemane asked our Lord what He had done with all the money that came from the lands that Mary sold at Magdala.

4. And the false accusation against our Divine Master was believed by, not a few, but by the majority of men. The bad believed it readily, and rejoiced that He was one of themselves. He had rebuked them, and warned them, and irritated them by His example; and crossed their trade of wickedness, and defeated their plans, and, it may be, had saved the innocent out of their hands. It was

joy to them that He could be blackened by accusation, which, however false, would still leave its stain, and never be forgotten. This was sharp enough. But it was worse when He saw that the good believed Him to be guilty: that they forsook Him, and shunned Him, and passed Him by. The animosity of immoral minds was easier to bear than the condemnation of the good; who, being deceived, believed what was said against Him. Then the rulers and guides of the people — the scribes and the priests, the men of strict observance and large knowledge of the law — they disapproved and discountenanced His exaggerated teaching and His unusual way of life: sometimes all night in prayer, sometimes eating and drinking with sinners. This Man, if He were a prophet, would know; but He does not know, therefore He is no prophet; and if not a prophet, then He is pretentious in His ways, and presumptuous in His condemnations even of the scribes who sit in the seat of Moses. Have any of the rulers of the people believed in Him? If not, no one should believe in Him. Many a good priest is criticised, censured, accused, condemned, loudly or in silence, and all that is said against him is believed and repeated. In the homes where he used to be welcome there is constraint. In the friends who used to greet him there is a distance. The falsehood has done its work, and no contradiction can ever overtake it. It follows him like a shadow; and it darkens his path wherever he goes. It has become a part of his public reputation; the majority believe it to be true. His brother priests believe it. His Bishop believes it, and does not clear him. The holy angels know it to be false. But the priest was predestined to be conformed to the image of the Son; and He was accused falsely, and men believed it to be true.

5. Lastly, our Divine Master died under the cloud of false accusation. He was never cleared of the reproach, though the witnesses could not agree together. What matter? The high priest and the scribes condemned Him, and the majority cried, "Crucify Him. What more need have we of witnesses?" His name was blackened, and He died upon the Cross deserted by friends, abandoned by men, and forsaken by God. He died as a malefactor between malefactors, in the sight of the multitude who once believed Him to be a prophet, and now believed Him to be a blasphemer. Even after His death this ill name survived Him. "This deceiver said, while He was yet alive." This same lot He left behind Him to them that are His. "God hath set forth us Apostles, the last, as it were, appointed to death. We are made a spectacle to the world, and to angels, and to men. We are fools for Christ's sake; but you are wise in Christ. We are weak; but you are strong. You are honourable; but we are without honour. Even unto this hour we both hunger and thirst, and are naked, and are buffeted, and have no fixed abode. And we labour, working with our own hands; we are reviled, and we bless; we are persecuted, and we suffer it. We are blasphemed, and we entreat. We are made the refuse of this world, the off-scouring of all even until now."[172] "The disciple is not above his master, nor the servant above his lord. If they have called the Master of the house Beelzebub, how much more them of the household." [173] Why should we complain if we be blackened with accusation, and

---

[172] 1 Cor. iv. 9-13.
[173] S. Matt. x. 24,25.

134

die under it? Innocence falsely accused is a close conformity to the Son of God.

Three thoughts, arising from all this, may give us both peace and strength when we are falsely accused. The first is, that innocence, suffering under sin, suffers for sinners. It is what S. Paul describes as "filling up those things that are wanting of the sufferings of Christ."[174] The sufferings of the Head redeemed the world. The infinite merits of the Cross have purchased all things for us. But the suffering of the mystical Body, and of every member of it, is united to the Passion of Jesus, and through Him it ascends, as an act of obedience, and patience, and self-oblation, to the Father.

The second thought is, that sinners are never so near their Divine Master as when they suffer innocently. S. Peter says: "Dearly beloved, think not strange the burning heat, which is to try you, as if some new thing happened to you; but if you partake of the suffering of Christ, rejoice that when His glory shall be revealed you may also be glad with exceeding joy. For if you be reproached for the name of Christ you shall be blessed; for that which is of the honour, glory, and power of God, and that which is His Spirit, resteth upon you."[175] If we are on our Lord's side we shall suffer both for Him and with Him. Wherever His Cross is, there He is also. Never so near as when we need Him most. Our shame, and pain, and burning of heart are the pledges of His nearness, and that He is opening our understanding to know what books

---

[174] Col. i. 24.
[175] 1 S. Pet. iv. 12-14.

cannot teach us. How often have we read the words, "A faithful saying: for if we be dead with Him, we shall live also with Him; if we suffer, we shall also reign with Him."[176] To be falsely accused is the last conformity of the servant to his Lord.

The third thought is, that our Divine Master has some greater work for us to do. He is fitting us for it by suffering, by taking away the sweetness, without which hirelings will not serve Him, by purifying our love from resentment against those who despitefully use us, and from all weak pity for ourselves. Till we have accepted our Master's lot, whose three companions, B. Angela of Foligno says, were Poverty, Sorrow, and Contempt, we shall not be worthy to be priests or soldiers of the Heart that was pierced. He gives to all His servants a measure of work according to their power. To the many He gives an easier task, to some a harder, to a few the hardest of all. All priests stand on Calvary; but some are nearer than others to His Cross. He measures out the share of His Cross as each can bear it. Some it touches only for a moment; on some it falls often; some have the prolonged lot of Simon of Cyrene; others have the mocking, others the vinegar and gall; some the desolation, and a few the false accusation under which He died. S. Romuald, S. Peter Martyr, S. Francis of Sales, S. Joseph Calasanctius, S. Vincent of Paul tasted this bitterness, and many more. It made them Saints, and fitted them for their work; for they were called to do the works of Saints. If, then, we have some share in this lot, it is a sure sign of His love and of His will to use us in some way as instruments of His

---

[176] 2 S. Tim. ii. 11,12.

power. Let us, then, never faint under it, nor fear, nor go about for human defenders, nor use human arts for our justification. Leave it to Him. "Commit thy way unto the Lord, and trust in Him, and He will do it; and He will bring forth thy justice as the light, and thy judgment as the noon-day."[177] When this token of His special service comes to you, give thanks. Say, *Benedicam Dominum in omni tempore.* I will bless the Lord in all times: in the time of peace, and in the time of trouble; in the time of gladness, and in the time of affliction; in the time when men trust me, and in the time when they mistrust me; in the time when they speak me fair, and in the time when they lay to my charge evil that I know not, and falsehoods that are believed as true.

CHAPTER XIII.

THE PRIEST'S FRIEND.

It is not to be denied that the life of a priest is a life of austere loneliness. From the day that he is set apart by ordination the words are true of him, "Without father, without mother, without genealogy, having neither beginning of days nor end of life; but likened unto the Son of God, a priest for ever."[178] He leaves home and friends; his birth and name and race are forgotten; no one asks where he was born, or cares where he may die. He is separated from the world, and never more alone

---

[177] Ps. xxxvi. 5,6.
[178] Heb. vii. 3.

than when he is in thronging streets and crowded rooms. It is true that he has his flock, his brethren in the priesthood, the whole visible Church, and all the Saints as his companions. But all this is not enough. There is a need of something nearer than this. Priests sometimes seek it in friendships, and in innocent relations of special intimacy. They need, as all men do, the *solatium humanitatis*. But in seeking it, or in accepting it, they often fall into a snare. "For by whom a man is overcome, of the same also he is the slave."[179] By whatsoever a man is overcome, by the same he is brought in bondage. There is no bondage greater for a priest than an unbalanced personal attachment. When he was ordained he gave his whole soul to his Divine Master; and in return he received the liberty which set him free from all inordinate friendships and all undue attachments. This liberty consists in a perfect equilibrium of his mind. It is poised on the love of God reigning over all his affections, perfecting them all in warmth and tenderness to all about him, but forbidding them so to attach themselves to any one as to lose their balance, or the perfect equilibrium of their mind. The sure signs of an unbalanced mind are frequent meetings, many letters, long visits, weariness at home, restless seeking, waste of time, impatience of solitude. When a priest finds his evenings tedious, his own room lonely, his books tasteless, it is clear that he has lost his equilibrium. He is in bondage to something or to some one, and he has lost his perfect liberty of heart. S. Jerome says: "Let the cleric who serves the Church of Christ first interpret his name, and, finding the definition

---

[179] 2 S. Pet. ii. 19.

of his name, let him strive to be what he is called. For if *cleros* in Greek is *lot* in Latin, clerics are, therefore, so called either because they are of the lot of the Lord, or because the Lord is their lot — that is, the portion of clerics. He, therefore, who is either himself the portion of the Lord, or has the Lord for his portion, ought so to live that he may both himself possess the Lord, and be possessed by the Lord. He who possesses the Lord, and says, with the prophet, 'The Lord is my portion,' can have nothing besides the Lord; for if he have anything besides the Lord, the Lord will not be his portion — *pars ejus non erit Dominus.*"[180]

"God spoke with Abraham as a man speaketh with his friend." Our Lord said: I call you not servants, but friends. The priest's friend is his Divine Master. And His friendship is enough. But it is enough only to those who rest on it alone. It cannot be mingled with lower friendships. It must reign in us as on a throne. Our Lord has promised to be "with us all days, even unto the consummation of the world." And He has ordained a way of personal presence, "above the order and conditions of nature," in which He is always with us. The priest's friend is Jesus in the most Holy Sacrament, abiding for ever in the midst of us; and the priest is with Him morning, noon, and night, in continual intercourse, and a perpetual relation of love and protection on the one side, and love and service on the other.

1. This divine friendship consists first, and above all, in an identity of will with His will.

---

[180] *De Vita Clericorum*, tom. iv. p. 259.

Friendship is defined as *idem velle idem nolle*. This identity comes from assimilation to Him. If we are like Him, we shall love and hate as He loves and hates. The same things will be to us bitter or sweet as they are to Him. "We, beholding with open face the glory of the Lord, are transformed into the same image from glory to glory, as by the Spirit of the Lord."[181] But a priest is to be the likeness of His Master to the world; and that likeness is a condition to the reception of Holy Orders. His will, therefore, ought to be identified with the will of his Lord. And so long as wills are identified friendships cannot fail. We well know what His will is for us. He wills "all men to be saved."[182] He wills our sanctification.[183] He wills that we trust Him altogether; that we not only say, but mean in all things, "Not my will, but Thine be done."

He wills also our happiness, and that with a divine longing, which exceeds all our inordinate cravings. The chief and governing desire of all men is to be happy. All their efforts are aimed at happiness, or rather at what they mistake for it, thinking that it will make them happy. But most men fail to obtain it, because they cannot discern the true from the false. Happiness is holiness. There is but one way to this one end; all other desires are deviations from happiness. He desires our happiness in the only true form and way. If we desire the same, then in this also we are of one will with Him. And this union being founded on a divine reality is eternal.

---

[181] 2 Cor. iii. 18.
[182] 1 S. Tim. ii. 4.
[183] 1 Thess. iv. 3.

2. Friendship is not only unity of will, but a mutual goodwill each to each. *Amicus alter ego. Sacerdos alter Christus.* The will of a friend is not only an austere goodwill, severely just. It is also a kindly will. Sometimes the truest friend is too high and exacting in his wisdom and conduct towards us. We trust him, but shrink from him. Not so our Divine Friend. He is kindly and pitiful; He knows our infirmities, and He meets them with the tenderness of compassion. We know that we are in His hands, and our whole life is ordered by Him. If He chastise us, it is because He loves us. He does not willingly afflict. It is only because affliction is necessary that He wills it for us. If it were not necessary it would not come. No unnecessary pain can come except by and from ourselves. When it comes He grieves over it. Without taking from us our freedom, and thereby reducing us from man to a machine, He could not protect us from ourselves. But all the discipline of sorrow and suffering which He wills for us, He wills in measure and proportion to our need. Less would not sanctify or save us. More than is needful will never come. We do not see as yet the end for which He is working, or the purpose of what He does. But His words to Peter were spoken also for our sakes: "What I do thou knowest not now, but thou shalt know hereafter."[184]

We know, too, that He wills for us all necessary good; that nothing in Providence or in grace will be wanting for our welfare in this life or for our eternal salvation. We are always exacting from Him the signs of His goodwill before we trust Him. But when we see proofs there is no room left

---

[184] S. John xiii. 7.

for confidence. When we are in straits and anxieties and see no human help, then is the time to trust Him. We read of those who in the depth of their need have knocked on the door of the tabernacle, asking for bread. A priest has this ready access to his Master in every time of need. He is the guardian of his Lord, who dwells under his roof or hard by in the sanctuary; and to Him be carries the account of all his troubles and cares personal and pastoral. All that befalls him, all his perplexities and perils and wants, be pours out to Him. The priesthood assures him that be is predestinated to be made conformable to the image of the Son, and therefore that all things will work together for his good under the guidance of a divine and loving will.

3. Once more, in friendship there is mutual service: not mercenary, nor stipulated, nor self-seeking; but generous, glad, and grateful. "Ye have not chosen Me; but I have chosen you, and have appointed you, that you should go and should bring forth fruit."[185] He was our Master before we were His servants; and He knew what He would do with us and by us. We are not our own, but already bought with a price. All we are is His. All faculties and powers of nature, all graces and gifts of the Holy Ghost, are His. A priest's whole life, if he be faithful to his priesthood and to himself, is, or may be, and therefore ought to be, a service to his Master. Even the common actions of our daily life are consecrated to Him, for we are wholly His. "Whether you eat or drink, or whatsoever else you do, do all to the glory of God."[186] "All whatsoever

---

[185] S. John XV. 16.
[186] 1 Cor. X. 31.

you do, in word or in work, all things do ye in the name of the Lord Jesus Christ; giving thanks unto God and the Father by Him."[187] This pervading motive, actual, virtual, or at least habitual, renewed morning by morning in Mass and after Mass, and through the day, especially in times of anxiety, danger, or temptation, is a continual service done for love and loyalty to our Divine Friend. How much more the sacred actions of our priesthood. The daily commemoration of Him with which the day begins; the oblation of His Sacred Heart, with all its adoration, for the glory of the ever-blessed Trinity; the offering of His precious Body and Blood, which redeemed the world and makes propitiation continually for the ever-multiplying sins of men, hastening the ascent of souls that are in expiation to the vision of peace; the feeding of the multitude with the Bread from heaven — all these acts of divine service to Him are fulfilled in every Mass we say. A day so begun can hardly end in waste and cold and the dim lights of this world. Why does not the fragrance and the fervour of our Mass sustain us through the day? It is the keynote, and all our hours ought to move in harmony. Every word spoken in God's name; every act, however small, done for our Lord's sake, consciously or in the habitual exercise of the priestly or pastoral office; every Sacrament administered, every declaration of the word of God, every soul sought and found, every sinner converted, every penitent sustained — all this is direct personal service rendered to our Divine Friend. Into this service, too, may be counted the conscientious use of time, patience under sorrows, humility under false accusation

---

[187] Col. iii. 17.

which no faithful priest will ever escape. And while our day is full of this service to Him, He is always serving us with more than a mutual fidelity. We little know how He guides and guards and compasses us about, and lays His hand upon our head when the fiery shafts of the wicked one fly thick around us. The dangers that we know are many; but many more those that are unknown. We pray God to deliver us from our secret sins; we have need to pray that He may deliver us from our secret dangers. There is a shield over us which is turned every way, as the assault comes upon us from all sides when we least know it to be near. Surrounded all day long by the world, good and bad, men and women, up-right and designing, open and false, happy is the priest who can return at night to the presence of his Master needing only to wash his feet. How many who go out *a latere Jesu* in the morning bright and peaceful have come back at night downcast and sad, with many memories unworthy of a servant and a friend. Still He is always the same. We vary and change and are overcast and lose our morning light. A blight and a tarnish fall upon us. But He is unchangeable in love, pity, and forgiveness. Before we lie down to rest He will absolve us from the failures and inconsistencies of the day. This sense of mutual service knits the bond which unites friends together.

4. Moreover, friendship is patient; but here is no reciprocity with our Divine Friend. Patience is all on His side. And His patience is inexhaustible. His countenance never changes. His Heart is always full of love. When we come back to Him He is as we left Him, for in Him there is neither variableness nor shadow of alteration. The Eternal Love is

immutable, and the deified human heart can never change. As He bore with the contentions, and rivalries, and ambitions, and slowness to believe in His first disciples, so He bears with us. Only they were not priests then, and we are. After their ordination they were soon restored to strength, and lifted above themselves. We begin with our priesthood and pastoral care, and we have still many of the faults which they had before they received their supernatural powers. And yet He dwells in the midst of us, silent and calm, seeing all our faults, yet blind to them; forgiving them, as He forgave Peter, with renewed commands to feed His sheep. His patience, too, is generous. He is easily satisfied. One word of self-accusation, of self-rebuke, of self-reproach, and all is past. We cannot and ought not to forget our unworthy words and actions, but He puts them behind His back. "He will not break the bruised reed, nor quench the smoking flax."[188] He waits in patience and in hope for our growth in perfection. And it is He that is the first to draw us to Himself before we have resolved to come. We fear and hesitate from conscious unworthiness, till an impulse of the will overcomes reluctance. It needs a firm conscience to examine itself truly. We see our faults without looking at them. To look is disquieting and humbling. It breaks our peace where there ought to be no peace till we have been open and honest with our good Master, who will easily forgive us if we do not so easily forgive ourselves.

5. Lastly, in friendship there is mutual society. When friends are united in love they are in

---

[188] Isaias xlii. 3.

union, even though they be as far as sunrise and sunset apart. The consciousness of united wills and mutual kindliness and mutual service and loving patience, with the memories of past days of affection and of happiness, makes the absent to be present, and those that are unseen to be all but visibly with us. Letters come and go and messages are interchanged, and we feel to share in all they desire, and we know that they share in all that belongs to us. Such is the society of human friendship, even when friends are parted far asunder. It is more sensible and active the nearer they are. In a household all are not always together, but all are conscious that all are under the same roof, and that they are one in heart and will. The friendship of a priest with his Lord is beyond all this in conscious nearness and conscious intimacy. We may go to Him at any hour. If He be silent, we know His meaning and His mind. He always welcomes us when we come to Him. He listens to all we say, and He consoles us by listening to our voice; for it is a relief to unburden our soul to a friend, though he answers not a word. We know that we have His sympathy; that He feels with us and for us; that all we say is noted and remembered; and that if He be silent now, the day is not far off when we shall hear Him say, "Enter thou into the joy of thy Lord."

No priest, then, is friendless. There is always one Friend in whom we may find perfect and changeless rest. Other friends often grieve and disappoint us. One only Divine Friend never fails. But our perception of His friendship will vary in the measure in which we maintain our liberty from all unbalanced human attachments. We owe our whole heart to Him from the hour of our ordination, and if we abide in this equilibrium we shall find His friendship alone enough. It is this craving for human sympathy that hinders our sense of the divine. S. Paul could say, *Cupio dissolvi et esse cum Christo*. Some of the servants of our Lord have prayed Him to stay His consolations as too great for them. They were detached from all creatures who so prayed. But in the measure in which we keep ourselves from all importunate and intrusive human friendships, which, being sensible, and visible, and always at hand, so easily steal away what is due to our Divine Friend, in that measure we shall find rest, and sweetness, and sufficiency in Him.

If we be weak and wander to human friendships, we shall soon find that there is no rest anywhere else. Everything else is too narrow for a soul to rest on; too changeful to be trusted; too full of self to give room for us. The priest who leans upon any human friendships, how holy soever they be, will soon find that instead of rest he has disquiet, instead of consolation a wearing and multiplying anxiety. *Quid enim mihi est in coelo, et a te quid volui super terram? Defecit caro mea, et cor meum; Deus cordis mei, et pars mea Deus in aeternum.*[189]

Do not let any one think that a priest who has one Divine Friend will be cold or heartless, or careless of flock and friends, of the lonely and the forsaken. The more united to his Master the more like Him he becomes. None are so warm of heart, so tender, so pitiful, so unselfish, so compassionate, as the priest whose heart is sustained in its poise and balance of supreme friendship with Jesus and in

---

[189] Ps. lxxii. 25,26.

absolute independence of all human attachments. His soul is more open and more enlarged for the influx of the charity of God. We are straitened not in Him, but in ourselves. As our hearts are so shall be the descent of the love of God. We shall be replenished as we can receive it. What S. Paul asked for all Christians at Ephesus is above all true of priests and pastors, "That you may be able to comprehend with all the Saints what is the breadth, and length, and height, and depth: to know also the charity of Christ, which surpasseth all knowledge, that you may he filled unto all the fulness of God."[190] No man will be so like Jesus in the three-and-thirty years of mental sorrow and human compassion as the priest in whose heart his Divine Master reigns alone.

---

[190] Ephes. iii. 18, 19.

CHAPTER XIV.

THE PRIEST AS PREACHER.

The Council of Trent teaches that preaching is the chief duty of Bishops.[191] S. Paul said of himself: "God sent me not to baptise, but to preach the Gospel."[192] For what is preaching? It is speaking to men in God's Name. It is to declare the Word of God.[193] It is to be ambassadors for Christ.[194] It is "the ministry of reconciliation," [195] the offer of salvation to men. "For whosoever shall call on the name of the Lord shall be saved. How shall they call on Him in whom they have not believed? or how shall they believe in Him of whom they have not heard? and how shall they hear without a preacher? and how shall they preach unless they be sent? As it is written: How beautiful are the feet of them that preach the gospel of peace, of them that bring glad tidings of good things."[196] How beautiful are the feet of the messenger coming "upon the mountains," as the prophet writes — that is, coming down with a message from the eternal hills.

In the beginning it was the Bishops alone who preached. The needs of the faith compelled them to delegate this, their chief office, to the priesthood. Dionysius the Areopagite calls them

---

[191] Sess. xxiv. De Ref. c. iv.
[192] 1 Cor. i. 17.
[193] 1 S. John i. 1-3.
[194] 2 Cor. v. 20.
[195] Ibid.
[196] Rom. x. 13-15.

therefore illuminators. They were then preachers, messengers, and evangelists. They were not pulpit orators.

1. The preaching of the Apostles was the voice of their Divine Master prolonged in all its majestic simplicity. The people "wondered at the words that proceeded out of His mouth." Surely "no man ever spoke like this Man." And yet a child could understand His words; they were as transparent as the light; they were few and persuasive. It was the intelligence of God Incarnate speaking to man in human speech. It was the Truth Himself in articulate words penetrating the intelligence of men. For brevity, simplicity, plainness, the words of Jesus are an example to preachers, as His life is an example to the pastors of His flock. We cannot conceive in our Divine Master the studied efforts of rhetoric or gesture. Calmness, majesty, and the might of truth were the attributes of His words to men.

The sermons of S. Stephen, S. Peter, S. Paul, in the Book of Acts prolong His divine voice. It may be truly said that in them He fulfilled His own promise. "He that heareth you heareth Me." So, again, in the Epistles of S. Paul, S. Peter, and S. John. The character of each comes out in their writings, but the brevity, simplicity, and plainness of their Master's teaching is still maintained. The absence of all art, of all self-conscious effort for effect, came from the consciousness of a divine message. The necessity that was laid upon them cast out all unworthy reflection upon themselves. S. Paul distinctly tells the Corinthians that he would use no arts of their rhetoricians, no imposing subtleties of their philosophers. There is an unspeakable power and grandeur in his few and simple words: "And I, brethren, when I came to you, came not in loftiness of speech or of wisdom, declaring unto you the testimony of Christ. For I judged not myself to know anything among you, but Jesus Christ, and Him crucified. And I was with you in weakness and in fear and in much trembling. And my speech and my teaching was not in the persuasive words of human wisdom, but in showing (demonstration) of spirit and power: that your faith might not stand on the wisdom of men, but on the power of God."[197] The weakness and fear and trembling arose from the consciousness of a divine mission of life and death. And his fear of human persuasion came from the intuition of faith, which told him that divine faith must stand on divine truth, and that the wisdom of man is not the word of God. Human oratory may generate human faith. Divine truth has a sacramental power which converts the soul to God.

2. The Apostles spoke out of a fulness of light and of fervour which was special and incommunicable, and that fulness had two causes. The first was that they had seen the Incarnate Word. "The Word was made flesh, and dwelt among us."[198] "That which was from the beginning, which we have heard, which we have seen with our eyes, which we have looked upon, and our hands have handled, of the Word of life. For the life was manifested; and we have seen and do bear witness, and declare unto you the life eternal which was with

---

[197] 1 Cor. ii. 1-5.
[198] S. John i. 14.

the Father, and hath appeared unto us."[199] "We have not followed cunningly devised fables when we made known to you the power and presence of our Lord Jesus Christ, but having been made eye-witnesses of His majesty."[200]

This gave to them a spiritual condition of mind which we call reality. What they declared they had seen: what they taught they had heard from His lips. They could not doubt, or hesitate, or qualify, or draw back before any contradiction. As S. Paul said, "If God be for us, who is against us?"[201] Their personal converse with our Lord, and their direct commission from Him, gave to their words and their life a momentum which nothing could arrest. Their preaching was the outpouring of their unchanging consciousness. Their whole soul, intellect, conscience, heart, and will went with every word. Their preaching was the testimony of an eyewitness and an ear-witness. It had in it a force beyond all words. Words rather hinder than help the directness and the power of truth when simply told by those who believe what they say. Men just delivered from some great danger, or coming from some terrible sight of death, use few words. If they use many, we feel that they have but little sense of what they have seen, and of what they are saying. They who had stood on Calvary and watched through the three hours, and they who saw Jesus after He rose from the dead, and S. Paul who saw Him till he was blinded by His glory, so long as life lasted must have been penetrated in every faculty

---

[199] 1 S. John i. 1.
[200] S. Pet. i. 16.
[201] Rom. viii. 31

and sense an fibre with the presence and the Passion and the love of Jesus. It must have been hard for them to hold their peace. They must have desired a hundred languages and voices and tongues to declare all day long the Passion on the Cross, the glory of the Resurrection, and the peace of the kingdom of God.

The other cause of the special power and force of the Apostolic preaching is also incommunicable — namely, the inspiration of the Day of Pentecost. "They were filled with the Spirit." The parted tongues of fire were emblems of the light and ardour with which they declared the Word of God to men. "Are not my words as a fire, and as a hammer that breaketh the rock in pieces?"[202] Such were the words of the Apostles, wheresoever they went in all the world.

We cannot conceive these messengers of the kingdom of God labouring to compose their speech or studying the rules and graces of literary style. The records of their preaching in the New Testament are artless and simple as the growths of nature in a forest, which reveal the power and the beauty of God. Their words and writings are majestic in their elevation, and depth, and pathos, and unadorned beauty, like the breadth and simplicity of the sea and sky. Their whole being was pervaded by the divine facts and truths, the eternal realities of which they spoke. They needed no preparation, no study, not even reflection. They spoke as their Master had spoken before them: "We speak what we know, and

---

[202] Jerem. xxiii. 29.

we testify what we have seen."[203]

3, But perhaps it will be answered that our state is so absolutely unlike, and so remote from theirs, that our preaching must be the result of preparation, study, and intellectual effort. To this the answer may be both yes and no. And first, in the affirmative. Not only is preparation needed for a preacher, but such preparation as perhaps goes far beyond what the objector intends. By preparation is commonly understood a carefully written composition, carefully committed to memory. It were well if all priests faithfully made such preparation. But the preparation required for a preacher goes farther back, and is deeper than this. It is the preparation, not of the sermon, but of the man. It is the remote, not the proximate, preparation which is chiefly needed. The man preaches, not the sermon, and the sermon is as the man is. S. Paul says, "We preach not ourselves, but Christ Jesus our Lord."[204] Now they who were full of His mind and presence could so preach, but no others can. Most men do preach themselves — that is, their natural mind — and the measure and kind of their gifts or acquisitions come out and colour and limit their preaching. The eloquent preach eloquently, the learned preach learnedly, the pedantic pedantically, the vain-glorious vain-gloriously, the empty emptily, the contentious contentiously, the cold coldly, the indolent indolently. And how much of the Word of God is to be heard in such preaching? Can it be said that such men "preach not themselves, but Christ Jesus our

---

[203] S. John iii. 11.
[204] 2 Cor. iv. 5.

Lord"? If our sermons are what we are, we must go a long way back in preparing to preach. The boy must preach, and the youth must preach, that the man may preach. It may be answered, S. Augustine was one of the greatest of preachers, but he began late in manhood. S. Augustine, like S. Paul, belongs to a special category, of which we will speak hereafter. The Church, in the Council of Trent, intends that from twelve years — the sacred age of the Divine Teacher in the Temple — boys tonsured, and in the cassock, "the habit of religion",[205] should be trained up in seminaries. Of these we will speak first; and we may say at once that we need in our proportion what the Apostles had in fulness. If we were full, as we ought to be, of the divine facts and truths of faith, we should never lack the matter; and if we were united, as we ought to be, in heart and will with our Divine Master, we should not lack either light or fervour.

But to return to preparation. If it is the man that preaches, preparation is a life; it must begin early. In boyhood we ought to learn our mother-tongue — no hard task, if those who teach us know it themselves; we ought also to learn early how to use our reason. There is nothing recondite or difficult in logic, nothing that boys could not learn as soon as they know their grammar. This remote preparation is radical and vital. Then in due time comes the knowledge of Holy Scripture, which explains the Catechism; and theology, which unfolds and develops the Catechism into the science of faith. These preparatory disciplines cannot be got up on occasion when wanted. They must have been

---

[205] Pontif. Rom. De Clerico faciendo.

wrought into the intelligence by a continuous and progressive formation.

There will always be exceptions to every law, even of nature. Among those who see, some are dim-sighted; among those who hear, some cannot discern the distinction of musical notes; so it may be true that among those who know, some may not be able to utter in speech what they know in thought. But these are exceptions, and may be set aside. Nervous agitation, want of self-command, fear, anxiety, desire to succeed, and the like often make men lose their self-possession. Then they stammer and forget. But as a law of our mind we may lay it down that whatever is really known can be surely said. *Verbaque praevisam rem non invita sequentur.* We think in words, and every thought clothes itself as it arises in the mind. If, then, we acquire the habit of thinking, we should acquire simultaneously a habit of mental utterance in words, and the utterance of the tongue would follow by a law of nature. The chief hindrance to this is the want of thinking. We read or copy the thoughts of other men, which, therefore, are not our own: we appropriate them by memory. But memory is not thought; and to think and to remember at the same time is a feat that few can accomplish. We may trust to memory altogether, or to thinking altogether; but the two mental processes impede each other, and cannot be safely combined. While men are remembering, thinking ceases; and when men think, memory is suspended. What need of memory when a man speaks out of the fulness of his present consciousness? It is a proverb that every man is eloquent on his own subject. Statesmen, lawyers, men of science, poets, soldiers, traders, each in his own craft, is ready and fluent at any time, howsoever sudden. They speak with facility and fulness. The habitual thoughts of each are upon his calling, work, or craft, and without preparation he is ready at any moment to speak correctly and promptly. Why is it, then, that a priest cannot without preparation speak for God and for His kingdom, for His truth and for His law? If we were full of these things, if we realised them and lived in them as the convictions of our reason and the affections of our hearts, to speak of them would be even a relief. We are never weary or embarrassed in speaking of those we love, and of the things that are dear to us. In the measure in which we realise the world of faith, the eternal truths, the nature of sin, the love of souls, their danger of perishing, we shall find no difficulty in speaking on them with sincerity and simplicity. It is the desire to be eloquent and to shine as orators that causes unreality, vainglory, and emptiness.[206] If we could only forget ourselves and speak seriously for God, we should find less difficulty in preaching; and the people would hear us gladly, because they would believe that we mean what we say. They are very quick to perceive, it may be said to feel, whether a priest speaks from his heart or only from his lips. The homilies of the early Fathers are unostentatious and full of Holy Scripture.[207] S. John Chrysostom might be quoted as florid in style; but it is not the self-conscious and stilted declamation which is praised as pulpit

---

[206] "Conturbatus qui siccatus: siccatus quia exaltatus." — S. Aug. serm. 131, tom. 7. p. 642.

[207] S. Jerome says: "Sermo Sacrarum Scripturarum lectione conditus sit. Nolo te declamatorem esse et rabulam." — Ep. ad Nepot. tom. iv. p. 262.

oratory. And S. John Chrysostom speaks in the style of S. Paul; and his mind was so like that of the Apostle that he was believed to write and speak with a special assistance from S. Paul. At all times preachers have been tempted to self-manifestation. We are told that when S. Bernard was preaching his sermon one day Satan said to him, "You have preached most eloquently;" and S. Bernard answered, "I neither began for thee nor will leave off for thee." We read, too, in the life of S. Vincent Ferrer that, having to preach before the King of France, he elaborated his sermon. It failed, and fell flat. The next day he preached again with little preparation. The King said to him, "Yesterday I heard Brother Vincent: to-day I have heard the Holy Ghost." It may, however, be truly said that pulpit oratory came in with the revival of paganism, impiously called the *Renascimento*. Men's heads were turned with literary vanity. The ambition to copy the Roman orators in style and diction and gesture destroyed the simplicity of Christian preachers, and bred up a race of pompous rhetoricians, frigid, pretentious, and grandiloquent. The evil, once in activity, spread, and has descended. Saints have laboured against it in vain — S. Ignatius with his energetic plainness, S. Philip with his daily word of God, S. Charles with his *virilis simplicitas* — his manly simplicity. But the flood had set in, and it bore down all opposition. The world runs after pulpit orators. They please the ear, and do not disturb the conscience. They move the emotions, but do not change the will. The world suffers no loss for them, nor is it humbled, nor wounded. We have not, indeed, seen our Divine Master, nor heard His voice; but if by faith and mental prayer we realise His presence, His truth, His will, and our own commission to speak in His name, we shall be filled with a consciousness of the unseen world and its realities, and out of that fulness we shall speak. We shall, indeed, need careful and minute preparation of what we are to say. But having a clear out- line in our intellect, words will by a law of our nature follow the spontaneous courses of our thought. But for this an accurate preparation of the subject matter with pen and ink, analysed and divided logically, with terms and propositions well defined, is absolutely necessary. Then this outline or synopsis must be thought out and impressed, not upon the memory, but upon the intellect, so that the whole, with its parts and its continuity, is present to the mind, not by remembering, but by reasoning. This kind of preparation requires more thought and mental industry than writing out a composition and learning it by heart. The difference between the two processes is this: the written sermon is what we thought when we wrote it; the spoken sermon is what we think at the moment of speaking. It is our present conviction of intellect and feeling of heart: it is therefore real, and felt to be real by those who hear. Happy are they who by such a discipline, intellectual and moral, identify themselves with the Word of God and speak it as their own.

We shall not indeed be inspired, but we know of no limit to the light and grace that God will give to those who ask it. He will give to us *os et sapientiam*, a mouth and wisdom in speaking for Him to the world. He is working His own purposes by us. We do not know to whom the message is sent. It often happens now that many years pass, and we know for the first time that on such a day and in such a place some word of ours has stung a conscience, or stirred a heart, or moved a will, and brought a soul to God. But we shall never know in this world all that God may have done while we were unconscious. Therefore, "Cast thy bread upon the running waters, for after a long time thou shalt find it again."[208] When we have made all such preparation as I have said, the last preparation is to kneel before our Divine Lord in the Blessed Sacrament, and to make the sign of the Cross upon our lips in honour of the Sacred Mouth, which spake as never any man spoke; offering to Him our confusion, if He be pleased to humble us by failure; and praying Him to work His own will by His own word, even though in our mouth. "He that heareth you heareth Me" gives us a share in the promise made in prophecy to Himself. "My Spirit that is in thee, and My words that I have put in thy mouth, shall not depart out of thy mouth, nor out of the mouth of thy seed, nor out of the mouth of thy seed's seed, from henceforth and for ever."[209] Therefore, "In the morning sow thy seed, and in the evening let not thy hand cease; for thou knowest not which shall rather spring up, this or that; and if both together, it shall be the better."[210]

With these words before us, what shall we say of a priest who catches up an old sermon, it may be, upon the Incarnation for Trinity Sunday, or on evil speaking for Christmas Day, or on heavenly joys in Lent; or, still worse, who goes to the pulpit without preparation, remote or proximate, without meditation and without prayer; who chooses his text

---

[208] Eccles. xi. 1.
[209] Isaias lix. 21.
[210] Eccles. xi, 6.

at the moment, trusting to a fluent tongue and a string of pious commonplaces? In the soul of such a priest can there be holy fear, a sense of the sanctity of God, of the account he must give for every idle word, or a love of souls, or a desire for the glory of God, or a consciousness that he is grieving the Holy Ghost?

CHAPTER XV.

THE PRIEST'S LIBERTY.

Has a priest more liberty than a layman? At first sight we say yes; because the office of the priesthood lifts him in privileges above other men, and makes him to be their judge and censor and guide. Moreover, he is rector of his mission or parish, and has a large discretion in all things: he is uncontrolled master of his own house, of his hours, of his habits, and, excepting in the discharge of his spiritual duties, he has the absolute control and disposal of his whole life. He may go where he will, stay as long as he likes, choose his own society. There is no one all day to check or to cross his liberty, and unchecked liberty easily grows to license. He is altogether independent of all except his Bishop, and his Bishop is at a distance. A priest is therefore, if any question arises, the judge in his own case. He decides and applies the law to himself. This is indeed a great and dangerous liberty, far beyond that of a layman.

Nevertheless a priest is under obligations from which the layman is free. He is hound in a special degree by the divine tradition of faith and morals, and that not only to observe it, but to make others to observe it. He is bound by the discipline of the Catholic Church, by the Pontifical law, which is partly common and universal, and partly the local law of the diocese to which he belongs. But beyond this he is bound by three chief obligations — that is, by the law of chastity, which is equivalent to a vow. And this obligation involves separation and abstinence from everything that can affect the inward purity of his soul, or withdraw his heart from the supreme love of his Divine Master. He can have no unbalanced human attachments. He is bound also to the spirit of poverty, and therefore to a life in the spirit of poverty. He may possess a large patrimony, and hold a rich benefice. He is not bound by law to give his patrimony to the poor. He may lawfully spend on himself and his house. But all things that are lawful are not therefore fitting or sacerdotal. Of his benefice he may take his due maintenance, but all beyond ought to go to pious uses. He may be rich, but if he would live as a priest, he ought to live as a poor man. If he live as a rich man, even though he commit no sin, he does not live like his Master. And the servant ought not to be above his Lord. In the measure in which he loves Him he will desire to be like Him, and will choose His lot.

Thirdly, he is bound to obedience. And that obedience has its rule in the laws of the Church and of the diocese, but it has its motive in the love of our Lord and of souls, and it has its obligation in the promise made in ordination in the hands of the

Bishop.

But beyond these obligations, which come by spontaneous contract in receiving the priesthood, there is a law and an obligation which binds every member of the mystical Body of Christ, and above all the chief members of the body — that is, the Bishops and priests of the Church — namely, the law of liberty. S. James says: "So speak ye and so do as beginning (or being) to be judged by the law of liberty."[211] This law is anterior to all other laws, bonds, or vows; it is universal, and constrains every regenerate soul. It is supreme, and has no limit in its requirements except the power we have to fulfil it.

S. Paul, writing to the Galatians, calls the law of Moses the law of bondage, and the Gospel the law of liberty. Writing to the Romans, he says that the law of bondage is the law of sin and death. But S. James has a higher meaning.

1. This law of liberty is, first, the law of God written upon our heart in our regeneration. By our first birth we were born in the bondage of sin and death. The knowledge of the law of God, and even of the existence of God, was obscured in us. By our regeneration we received from the Holy Ghost the virtues of faith, hope, and charity. Baptism was called φωτισμoσ, and the baptised illuminated.[212] The knowledge of God and of His law was restored to us. The will, which was wounded and weakened by original sin, was liberated from the bondage of weakness and restored to its liberty. It was this that

---

[211] S. James ii. 12.
[212] Heb. X. 32.

God promised, when He said: "This is the testament which I will make with them after those days, saith the Lord. I will give My laws in their hearts, and in their minds will I write them."[213]

By our regeneration we are made sons of God. By the infusion and indwelling of the Holy Ghost the will is elevated and empowered to do the will of God. By our first birth it was deprived of the Holy Ghost. By our second birth the will is invested once more with supernatural power. "As many as received Him to them He gave power to become sons of God." The weakness of the will and the strength of passion brought the will into a bondage. It had always its freedom, but it was bribed by its lower affections to betray itself. By our regeneration we enter into the liberty of the sons of God. S. Paul describes this: "There is now, therefore, no condemnation to them that are in Christ Jesus, who walk not according to the flesh; for the law of the spirit of life in Christ Jesus hath delivered me from the law of sin and of death."[214] They are set free from the guilt of original sin: from its power, and from its fascination. The chief danger in sin is its sweetness and its subtlety. It fascinates and deceives the soul. It draws by desire and it deceives by its dissimulation. There is no duty of a son of God that the regenerate cannot fulfil if they have the will. They have both the power and the freedom. This, then, is the first step in the liberty of the children of God. They are free from eternal death. It has no claim or power over them; nor can it regain its power unless they betray themselves.

---

[213] Ibid. x. 16.
[214] Rom. viii. 1,2.

2. Further, the law of liberty is the will elevated by the love of God. To serve God is to reign. To love God is perfect liberty. *Ubi spiritus Domini ibi libertas.*[215] *Charitas Dei diffusa est in cordibus nostris per Spiritum Sanctum, qui datus est nobis.*[216] Where the Spirit is, there is liberty; for the Spirit of God is love, and where love is, there is liberty. There can be no liberty where love is not. Where the love of God is not, the love of creatures, and of the lowest of all creatures, the love of self, reigns. There can be no greater bondage than this. The love of creatures brings with it jealousies, disappointments, resentments, and manifold temptations. A priest who has lost his liberty by any unbalanced attachment is in bondage. He is dependent for his happiness and for his peace upon something below God, which is changeful, uncertain, and transient. S. Augustine describes his own state, before the supreme love of God set him free, as a bondage of iron chains, not forged by the hands of other men, but by his own iron will.

But afterwards, when he had been redeemed into the liberty of the sons of God, he said, "Love and do what you will;" for our will then is the will of God. We have no other will than His, and in doing His will we do our own. For love is the will, and the will is love. *Pondis voluntatis amor.* As we love so we will. Love inclines the will, and gives it motion and momentum. It is by love that we cleave to God. *Qui adhaeret Domino unus spiritus est.*[217] This unity is unity of will. And it is known to ourselves, and shown to the

---

[215] 2 Cor. iii. 17.
[216] Rom. v. 5.
[217] 1 Cor. vi. 17.

world by many sure and evident signs. First, it changes all our aims in life. Before, we were aiming at many things below God; things, it may be, evil and dangerous, or things innocent and lawful, yet below God. We were full of them, and we shaped our life so as to insure them. Now we have aims altogether new. Our aspiration is for nothing on this side of the horizon, but beyond it. The kingdom of God, and God Himself; the vision of God, and union with Him: these are the aims which govern our life.

And as our aims so our interests — that is, the governing desires of our daily life and work. Once it was for the fair, and innocent, and lawful things of this world — for of other and darker things we are not speaking now — for many things we lived, and toiled, and spent our strength, till a higher light fell upon us, and the love of God arose in our hearts. Thenceforward we turned our whole mind and will to deeper and austerer works. The salvation of souls, the spread of the faith, the extension of the kingdom of God, the hallowing of His name, the reign of His will in all around us: these became the interests which absorbed all our thoughts and efforts. We ceased to be of those who seek their own things, and became of those who seek "the things that are Jesus Christ's."[218]

To these new aims and new interests are added also new tastes — that is, new interior and spiritual perceptions of pleasure and delight in things which in time past were, for us, without sweetness or attraction; as, for instance, prayer, the

---

[218] Philip. ii. 21.

reading of Holy Scripture, the Holy Mass, the solitude of the sanctuary, when we are alone in His presence; or in anything we can do for His sake, however slight; or in self-denial, when we can make a greater effort in His service. These are the things of the Spirit of God which are foolishness to the mind which judges by intellect and by sense alone. Everything we shrank from then becomes attractive. Crosses, disappointments, vexations, losses, which are a slight tasting of the sharpness and sadness of His lot, become to us pledges of His love and proofs of our fidelity to Him.

3. Lastly, the law of liberty is the will become a law to itself. "The law was not made for the just man,"[219] but for the disobedient. "Love is the fulfilling of the law."[220] "He that loveth his neighbour hath fulfilled the law." [221] Love anticipates all commandments. It instinctively and promptly and fully does what the law constrains the unwilling to do.

S. John says: "Whosoever is born of God committeth no sin, for His seed abideth in him, and he cannot sin because he is born of God."[222] That is, the Holy Ghost, the Sanctifier, dwells and reigns in him; and his whole new nature, which is spiritual and supernatural, revolts at sin in all its forms and fascinations. Without violence, and a violation of his whole mind, he could not sin: it would not be against God only, but against his own will. If it were

---

[219] 1 S. Tim. i. 9.
[220] Rom. xiii. 10.
[221] Ibid. xiii. 8.
[222] 1 S. John iii. 9.

put before such a will to commit a mortal sin or to die, it would willingly die. If it had to choose between a deliberate venial sin or to die, it would rather die. If it were bidden to choose a lot in life with equal hope of salvation, the one without the Cross, the other with the Cross, it would choose the Cross out of a desire of greater conformity to our Divine Master, and from gratitude for His sufferings for us, and from generosity of love to Him.

The law of liberty, then, is the law which moved God *liberrimo consilio* by His most free counsel of wisdom, to create us,[223] and to give His Son for our redemption. It moved the Son to take upon Him our manhood, and to offer Himself of His own will for us upon the Cross. *Oblatus est quia ipse voluit.*[224] It was the law of liberty that moved the ever-blessed Trinity to predestine, to call, to justify, to glorify us by the adoption of sons; to call us to the priesthood, to make us the first-fruits of the first-fruits of the Spirit. As all things are for His glory, so He ordained us for His greater and for His greatest glory. All this was without necessity or constraint. It was done only and altogether of the free will of God; for the will of God is His wisdom and His love in one perfect act, and His wisdom and love are His law. He is the law to Himself. Law and liberty are distinct, but indivisible. And this law of liberty was manifested to the world in the Incarnate Word. In Jesus Christ we see a will that is a law to itself; and all who are like Him in the measure of their likeness become their own law in the use of their liberty. This law leaves behind it all literal commandments,

---

[223] Concil. Vat. Const. Dogm. De Fili Cat. c. i.
[224] Isaias liii. 7.

as the learned becomes unconscious of the alphabet, and the skilful singer unconscious of the octave. It is a law more constraining that any commandment. It moves the heart, and urges the conscience, and prompts the will by a continuous pressure. By this law we shall all be judged; but, above all, by this priests will have to answer.[225]

We ought, then, to live by it now. In all our life we have never done wrong but we might have done right. The liberty and the power were with us. Again, we never left the right undone but we might have done it. We have never done right but we might have done better. We correspond with a few graces out of a multitude, and with inadequate fidelity, and with intermittent efforts. All these are failures in the law of liberty.

What motive, then, is there wanting to constrain a priest to the highest aspiration? We all are bound by the law of nature to obey our Maker with the utmost powers and affections of our whole being; by our redemption we are bound to glorify our Redeemer, for He has bought us for Himself. By our regeneration we are bound to obey the Holy Ghost as sons of God; by faith we are bound to obey the revealed law of God; by hope, to use all means of attaining eternal life; by charity, to love Him *super omnia*, with our whole soul and strength. This is true of all. But priests are bound beyond all men — by their higher predestination, by their greater grace, by the unction and character of their priesthood, by

---

[225] "Si reddenda est ratio de iis quae quisque gessit in corpore suo, quid fiet de iis quae quisque gessit iu corpore Christi quod est Ecclesia." — Inter Opp. Sti. Bern. Ad Praelatos in Concilio.

their participation in the character and priesthood of the Son of God, by the commission and charge He has given to them, and by the promises they have made to Him, by their love as disciples and friends, by gratitude, and by generosity — to use their liberty, not grudgingly or by constraint, but with gladness, joy, and self-oblation, even with denial and sacrifice of self in its fairest and most innocent forms, if need so be, that they may serve Him more perfectly in saving the souls for whom He died. "All things are lawful to me," but I will not therefore do or enjoy all that is lawful, for "all things are not expedient." They will not advance my salvation, my sanctification, my sacerdotal perfection. "All things are lawful to me, but all things edify not." If, by my example, I mislead any one, or embolden any one to do with danger to himself that which is no danger to me, or if I relax his perseverance or lower his aspiration, or if, by my unconscious influence, I undo what I have tried to teach to others, or give them scandal, then the use of my liberty, however lawful, will be not only not expedient, but a hindrance to their salvation, and still more to my own.

Happy is the priest who offers up his whole liberty to his Master, and restricts it generously in all his contact with the world. If we must go into it, we need to have continually in our ears the words, *Quid hic agis, Elia?* The priest who is seldom seen in society is the priest whom men desire most to have beside them when they die. S. Jerome says of priests: *Si quis saepe invitatus ad convivia non recusat, facile contemnitur.* Our Lord did indeed go to the house of Simon, and to the marriage in Cana. But everywhere He was the Son of God. He went nowhere but by divine charity. If we use our liberty for Him as He used His for us, we shall live in the world to save it, but live out of the world to save ourselves. Priests and pastors have a special need of protection: and also a special promise of safety so long as they use their liberty for His sake with generous abnegation of self. "Holy Father, keep them in Thy name whom Thou hast given Me. While I was with them I kept them in Thy name. Those whom Thou hast given me have I kept; and none of them is lost but the son of perdition. I pray not that Thou shouldst take them out of the world, but that Thou shouldst keep them from the evil."[226]

Our Lord used His liberty to die for us. And this He did to redeem us and to win back our love. We use our liberty to live for ourselves. S. Paul describes the perilous times of the last days by a list of sins, chiefly spiritual, and he winds it up by saying that men will be "lovers of their own selves:" "lovers of pleasures more than lovers of God."[227] He says in another place that "all men seek the things that are their own, and not the things that are Jesus Christ's:"[228] that is to say, they are sinners, who break the laws of God; or worldly, in whom the love of the Father is not; or self-seekers, who have an end in everything, whether in high ambitions or in petty gains; or selfish, who with a sectarian spirit care nothing for others — the fraternity of Cain, who first said, "Am I my brother's keeper?" So long as they have a seat in church and get their confessions heard, they have no care for the sheep. Souls may

---

[226] S. John xvii. 11, 12, 15.
[227] 2 S. Tim. iii. 4.
[228] Philip. ii. 21.

perish all around, but it does not matter to them. Finally, among those who seek their own are the spiritual gluttons, who crave intensely after the consolations and enjoyment of religion, which they would speedily forsake if they were not allured like children. Those that seek the things that are Jesus Christ's are the innocent and the penitent, the disinterested, the self-denying, the good soldiers who endure hardness and the Cross in their zeal for souls, for the Church, and for the priesthood. The first use their liberty for themselves; the last, for their Master. In one of these two categories every priest will be; for there is no neutrality where loyalty is a duty: and there is nothing but lukewarmness between cold and hot.

There are five signs of the wise and generous use of our liberty.

(1) The first is not to be content unless we return Him love for love. He has loved us with an everlasting love before we were, and with a personal love when we came into the world, and with a redeeming love in our regeneration, and with a love of friendship since we came to know and to love Him. What love can we offer Him in return but a love above all things with our whole soul and strength? How can we be so self-satisfied when we read: "If any man love not our Lord Jesus Christ, let him be anathema maranatha"?[229] And again: "No man can say, the Lord Jesus, but by the Holy Ghost."[230] His love and His service are high and

---

[229] 1 Cor. xvi. 22.
[230] Ibid. ii. 3.

austere realities.

(2) The second sign is zeal for Him; that is, an unresting and ardent desire to use all time, and faculties, and means for the fulfilment of His will, for the spread of His truth, for the honour of His name, for the service of His Church, for the saving of souls.

(3) The third is a sorrow with Him and for Him, because of the sins committed by those who do not know Him, and, still more, by those who do, against the faith, against the unity of the Church, against its authority, against His love by ingratitude, against His person by sacrilege, against His pastoral care by scandals which destroy the souls for whom He died. The sight of souls perishing within and without the Church, to those who have love and zeal, will be a daily sorrow.

(4) The fourth is generosity in giving ourselves and giving up our liberty in anything we can do or sacrifice for His sake, spending and being spent for the elect's sake.[231]

(5) The fifth is a joy in crosses. They may be of three kinds. First, those that are deserved for our faults, for our imperfections, and for our past sins. Secondly, for those we have not deserved, as false accusation, contempt, and hatred without a cause. Thirdly, those that are voluntary— that is, incurred by any acts or restriction of our liberty which may offend those who indulge their liberty too much.

---

[231] 2 Cor. xii. 15.

The stream of the whole Christian world at this day is running fast to a liberty which ends in license. It is the time-spirit and the downward course of these last days. We are so acclimatised to a soft self-sparing life that we interpret even the words of the Holy Ghost till they become colourless and metaphorical. Who now takes as a rule of life the words, "God forbid that I should glory save in the Cross of our Lord Jesus Christ, by whom the world is crucified to me and I unto the world."[232] What sign of crucifixion is there in our blameless easy life? Or again, "With Christ I am nailed to the Cross; and I live, not now I, but Christ liveth in me. And that I now live in the flesh, I live in the faith of the Son of God, who loved me and delivered Himself for me."[233]

What marks of the nails are there in our free life, and what sign of Christ reigning in us and through us upon all our words and actions? We seem to read the law of liberty backwards: "So speak ye and so do as they who, if they do not willingly sin, need not deny themselves in anything;" instead of "So speak ye and so do as they who desire to restrict their liberty in all things, that they may be conformed to the Son of God, who denied Himself for us."

---

[232] Gal. vi. 14.
[233] Ibid. ii. 19, 20.

CHAPTER XVI.

THE PRIEST'S OBEDIENCE.

We have seen what is the priest's liberty. So long as he does not violate the obligations of his priesthood and the discipline of the Church, he has as much liberty as any other man. But if he use his liberty like other men, he will not be able to say to his flock, "Be ye followers of me as I also am of Christ."[234] A priest who lives up to the limits of his liberty is a lax priest, and a lax priest is an unhappy man. He is fenced all round with restrictions, and they gall him because he does not love them. He has upon him the yoke of the priesthood, which frets him because it is not his joy. The happiest of men is a strict priest, to whom the yoke of the priesthood is sweet, and its restrictions far less than the limitations he has of his own free will imposed upon his liberty. Now what is it that makes a difference even among good men between priest and priest? They have equally the three characters of sons, soldiers, and priests of Jesus Christ, and they have in their measure and proportion the sacramental graces which flow from them. In what do they, then, differ? The difference would seem to be in the use the one makes and the other does not make of the seven gifts of the Holy Ghost which are in him. The virtues of faith, hope, and charity are habits; but the gifts are faculties or powers which elicit and perfect these virtues. Three of the gifts — fear, piety, and fortitude — perfect the will; four perfect the reason: intellect and science perfect the speculative reason;

---

[234] 1 Cor. iv. 16.

counsel and wisdom perfect the practical reason. These seven gifts, when fully unfolded, make men to be saints; unfolded partially and unequally they make the diversities of sanctity seen in the Church; or good, but not perfect, Christians. In the measure in which they are unfolded they give a special character to the mind. Some priests are skilled in counsel, some in intellectual subtlety some in piety, some in courage, and the like. It is not often that we see all the seven gifts equally unfolded in the same character, for it would form a saintly mind, and saintly minds are few.

But this gives us the key of the great diversities among good priests. Some are wise but not learned, some learned but not pious, some pious but not courageous. Now theologians tell us that it is the loss of these gifts that makes men foolish. When both the reason and the will are imperfectly unfolded, the whole character shows it. Some etymologists derive *stultitia* from stupor, and they tell us that *stultitia* is *luxuriae filia*, the offspring of a soft and indulgent life. We see even in good priests, whose life is untaxed by effort, leisurely, easy, regular, and blameless, a tendency to inertness and tardiness of mind.

So also in men of the world. The intellectual conceit, indocility, and independence in matters practical and speculative come from the neglect of the gifts of intellect and of counsel. Men of science are especially liable to this dwarfed and distorted intellectual habit. But we have nothing to do with them now; we are speaking of priests — that is, of ourselves. The reason why sometimes priests are pretentious, vain, scornful, critical, and their preaching unconvincing and unpersuasive, may be found in the same cause. As the loss of the seven gifts produces stupor of mind at least in spiritual things, so the obstructing them in their development and neglecting them in their exercise produces insensibility and inaccuracy. Holy fear is the beginning of wisdom. It is a great gift, and keeps us from evil; but without piety we shall be at least cold and hard to others. Filial piety is the loving and tender affection of a son, but without fortitude it may become soft and unstable. If these gifts, which perfect and govern the will, are obstructed or weakened in their action, a priest will be a feeble support to those who need his help. So if his practical reason be warped or darkened, he will be an untrusty teacher of his flock; and if his speculative reason be clouded, he will be an unsafe guide for the innocent, the penitent, and the doubtful.

There are five things which will cherish and unfold the working of the seven gifts in us. The first is a spirit of penance — this clears away the obstructions and hindrances which clog and defeat the working of the Spirit; the second is a constant study of Holy Scripture, for in it the Holy Ghost speaks and perfects His own work in us; the third is a daily prayer for light, in the beginning of the day, in the beginning of our studies or of grave actions; the fourth is mental prayer, by which our conscious union with God, and our consciousness of His presence in us, is kept alive; the fifth and last is a spirit of docility, a sense of dependence on God for light, guidance, strength, shelter, and safety; and an ear to hear His voice in our conscience, with a promptness to obey when His voice is heard. A docile mind is always saying: "My heart is ready, my heart is ready;" "Speak, Lord, for Thy servant heareth." These five habits will continually unfold the seven gifts in our intellect and our will, and form in us the habit of mental obedience, the *rationabile obsequium*, without which a priest cannot be *alter Christus*, or the likeness of his Master.

We will therefore try to see more carefully in what this mental obedience consists.

1. First, it consists in a loving obedience to the Church. Obedience without love is a mask, not a living reality. To obey because we must, to obey for fear of penalties or censures, is not enough. The obedience of our Lord in His baptism is our example. Why was He, the sinless Son of God, baptised with a sinner's baptism? Why was He, the greater, baptised by the less, the Lord by the servant? Why was He baptised in the sight of His enemies, as if He were as they thought Him to be — a sinner, and a friend of sinners? It was that He might fulfil all justice; that humility and obedience to His Father might have their perfect work. What plea, then, can a priest ever find for disobedience? The rule, or the injunction, he may say, is needless, irksome, open to misunderstanding, emanating from an authority partial or ill informed. Be all this true, yet the duty and grace of obedience remain unchanged, and a docile mind will obey. They who criticise authority are not docile. Even if they obey, they lose the grace of obedience; if they disobey, they must give account to God. The mind that was in Christ Jesus is the mind of obedience; and the mind of the Divine Head pervades the Body of Christ. The axiom, *Sentire cum Ecclesia*, means also to

believe with the Church, to hope with the Church, to love with the Church, and therefore to obey with the Church. A priest is, above all, *vir obedientiarum*, a man of many obediences. He obeys the Father as a son, the Son as a priest, the Holy Ghost as a disciple, the Church as his mother, the Bishop as the visible witness and representative of all these, who, in God's name, receives his obedience in the person of Jesus Christ. Such an obedience dignifies a priest. It is the highest act of his will. It matters not whether the obedience be in a great thing or in a small. The same authority runs through all the commandments and laws of discipline, and speaks to us by the living voice of Him to whom we have promised obedience. Prudence is his duty, obedience is ours. Mental obedience does not argue, or object, or criticise. It obeys; and in his obedience a Divine Presence meets the priest, and blesses him. The absence of such mental obedience betrays the absence of the gift of wisdom.

2. Another sign of mental obedience or docility is devotion to the Saints. They are our examples. Their counsels, their sayings, their instincts, are our rule and admonition. S. Philip bids us read authors who have S. before their name. They were once what we are now, weak, buffeted, tempted, penitent, and even sinful. We shall be hereafter, if we persevere to the end, what they are now. Their examples come home to us in every state of life, and in every part of our spiritual warfare. They are planted all along our path, in every age and condition, as guides and admonitions. In their lives we see the commandments, the precepts, and the counsels embodied. Every devout priest has his patrons. A priest without an intimate

relation to Patron Saints can have little realisation of the supernatural order in which we live, and of our communion with "the spirits of the just made perfect."[235] It is not enough for a priest to have devotion to our Blessed Mother. She is not the patron of any one, being the Mother of all. Our relation to her is necessary, not voluntary. We cannot have God for our Father without having the Church for our Mother; and we cannot have God for our Father without having the ever-blessed Mother as our Mother. We do not choose her as a patron. We are her children from our baptism, before we knew her, in the supernatural consanguinity of the Incarnation. So, also, we hardly choose S. Joseph; for he is the patron of the universal Church. We, therefore, are his foster-children through the maternity of the spotless Virgin Mary. Our patrons are of our own choosing. And a priest must be of a strangely unreflecting mind who does not find himself in manifold relations to "the Church of the first-born written in heaven."[236] The day or place of our birth, our falls, our faults, our needs, our works, all suggest to us many who, in their warfare on earth, were tried as we are. The habit of mind that turns to the Saints is a docile reverence; the habit of mind that turns away from them is an indocile self-sufficiency. Devotion and conscious relation to the Saints is a part of the gift of piety. It is the affection of mind by which we adore the ever-blessed Trinity with our whole soul and strength; for love and worship are the same affections, whether the object be infinite and uncreated, or finite and a creature. But this

---

[235] Heb. xii 23.
[236] Heb. xii. 23.

charity differs infinitely in motive and in measure. The worship of God has no measure in us except our finite nature, because of His immensity. The worship of the Saints is finite, because they are creatures. The love of our neighbour begins with our kindred, and ascends continually from earth to heaven, from our homes to the heavenly court. It was well said by one who saw the truth in part that "the greatest school of mutual respect is the Catholic Church." He saw that the reverence of children to their parents, of subjects to their rulers, of people to their priests, of priests to their Bishops, of Bishops to the Head of the Church, is all one habit of mind, differing only in measure and accidental diversities. In itself it is all one habit of filial piety. A priest who is devout to the Saints will hardly be irreverent and contumacious, or critical and murmuring against his superiors. France has been infected and afflicted by a spirit of mockery against all authority, sacred or secular. England has hitherto been free. But everywhere there will be whisperers, murmurers, critics, censors, and carpers, who spare nobody, and least of all those whom they should most respect, if not for what they are, at least for the office they bear. Such minds invoke their own Nemesis. No priests are so carped at as they who carp at their brethren; none are so turned into ridicule as those who ridicule superiors. Carping in a priest betrays the absence of the gift of piety.

3. A third sign of mental obedience is deference to theologians. It is true that we incur the note of heresy only when we impugn the faith; but we may incur the notes of error, rashness, offensiveness to pious ears, in rejecting opinions which are outside of divine or Catholic faith. Private

judgment, three hundred years old and erected into a law, and even into a religion, has infected the atmosphere in which the Catholic Church is forced to live and to breathe. It is true that the teaching of theologians, even though unanimous, will not make matter of divine faith; but their consent creates an intellectual tradition against which no man can set his judgment without rashness. We should be rash if we measured ourselves against any one of them; we should be more than rash if we set ourselves against their unanimous judgment. The unanimous interpretation of the Fathers makes a rule for fixing the sense of the Scriptures against all private spirits. The unanimous teaching of theologians is the maximum, or a high degree of human certainty in matters of revealed and of unrevealed truth. If we trust our individual reason, is not their collective reason to be rather trusted? If we think that the light of the Spirit of Truth has been leading us, does He not also lead them? And is not their unanimity the result of a collective guidance and a confluent illumination? Their combined and united light puts out our isolated spirit, as the noonday sun makes all lesser lights to be invisible. The habit of teaching others generates also a habit of forming and adhering to our own opinion. We are sent to affirm and to assert, and this leads easily to self-assertion. The teachers of dogma easily become dogmatic. Priests meet with less of contradiction than other men, and often bear it less patiently. Men in the world, as at the Bar, or in Parliament, are trained by constant contradiction to courtesy and forbearance. They are often an example and a rebuke to us. It is the absence of the gift of counsel that makes us opinionated and impatient.

4. Another sign of mental obedience or docility is a fear and suspicion of novelties in doctrine or practice or devotion. Theology or the science of God is a divine tradition, running down from the beginning, ever expanding, and rising in its unity and symmetry to perfection. It is built up indeed of things old and new, but the new are, as Vincent of Lerins said, *non nova sed nove*. The coins of the Roman, the Byzantine, the British Empire have new and various images and superscriptions, but the gold is all one. So the definitions of the truth may be new, but the truth is old. It is the restless sea of human intellect casting up mire and darkness that forces the Church to make new dykes, and to guard the faith with new definitions. But some minds are weary of old truths, old terms, old phrases, old modes of teaching, old prayers, old devotions. They need the stimulus of novelty: new colours, new forms, new ways of stating old doctrines. It is with doctrines as with fashions: they must be always changing. Critics and authors, professors and preachers, often have a craving for originality. To be like their forefathers is to be commonplace; to strike out new lines, new ways of putting old truths, makes a reputation. It is only the Church that can revise the sacred terminology of faith. It alone "can bring forth things old and new," All other innovations are departures from the beaten path, which is safe because beaten, and beaten because it is the way of our forefathers in the faith. What is true in theology is more evidently true in the interpretation of the sacred Scripture. The love of novelty is always at work to find new meanings; and criticism is impatient of restraint. We live in an age of unlimited intellectual liberty. Priests read without scruple or hesitation books and writings which fall

under the rules of the Index. The habit of intellectual independence is easily formed. We are surrounded by both Gnostics and Agnostics: by those who out of their own consciousness are wiser than the Church, and by others who measure what can be known by what they know. Catholics would not consciously listen to either of these schools of error; and yet they are continually and unconsciously taking in their erroneous premises, and principles, and assumptions in their daily contact with the world. As to false theology and false interpretation of Scripture, they would be upon their guard; but they are off their guard in philosophy, and readily open their ears and their intellect to the aberrations of modern metaphysics. They think that as in philosophy there is no heresy, so there need be no fear. But a false philosophy undermines faith, and one philosophical error, like a rotten beam, will loosen the whole superstructure of theology. Priests have of all men need to be upon their guard, for they are the guides and teachers of the faithful. It is dangerous to receive and to propagate the least intellectual error. We have need to live in great watchfulness against what is glorified as "modern thought." The thought of the modern world is setting steadily away from God. The love of novelty is one of its signs, and the only adequate corrective is the *donum scientiae*, the gift of science or knowledge, which sees God in all things, and all things in God. With this light we may traverse the whole world of abstract or applied sciences without hesitation or fear.

5. There remains still one more sign to be added, that is, a mistrust of self in all its forms, especially in our intellectual and moral judgments.

To acquire this self-mistrust we have only need to remember three things — first, how often we have erred in our opinions; secondly, how little we have read; thirdly, how little we have studied. To read is one thing, to study is another. No conscientious priest will shut his books; no wise priest will answer in grave matters without consulting them; no priest who mistrusts himself will print and publish without putting his book under the revision of other eyes and other minds; the more the better. We must know how to learn before we teach. And we must learn to obey before we can guide. This mistrust of self comes from the gift of filial fear — that is, the fear of offending God either in His law or in His truth by any reckless action or by any idle word.

It is to priests emphatically that S. John's words apply: "Ye have an unction from the Holy One, and you know all things." And among those things are, first and above all, the knowledge of God and the knowledge of self, out of which springs mistrust of self. It was of our Divine Lord, whose priesthood we share, that Isaias prophesied: "The spirit of the Lord shall rest upon Him; the spirit of wisdom and of understanding, the spirit of counsel and of fortitude, the spirit of knowledge and of godliness. And He shall be filled with the spirit of the fear of the Lord."[237] Of this unction every priest receives, and in the measure in which these seven gifts are cherished by conscious obedience he is conformed to his Divine Master.

---

[237] Isaias xi. 2, 3.

CHAPTER XVII.

THE PRIEST'S REWARDS

The Prophet Isaias foretold of the Man of Sorrows that He should have His consolation in the midst of suffering: "Because His soul hath laboured, He shall see and be filled;"[238] that is, He shall see the fruit of His toils and tears even upon earth. So with His servants. In the midst of all his sorrows and labours, anxieties and disappointments, a priest has a multitude of consolations; even in this life he has a great recompense of reward. God will not be outdone in generosity. Whosoever forsakes anything for His sake, He will repay a hundredfold. What S. Paul said to all the faithful is emphatically true of priests. They who strip themselves of all things for Christ's sake, in the measure in which they are poor thereby become rich: *nihil habentes, omnia possidentes.*[239] Again he says, "All are yours, and ye are Christ's, and Christ is God's."[240] The legal earthly rights of the rich in this world in no way bar the enjoyment of the faithful. The earth is the Lord's and the fulness thereof.[241] And through "the Heir of all things" we inherit all things. The earth, sea, and sky were made before the human laws of property existed. A priest who has nothing but his bare sustenance enjoys without burden or responsibility all the works of Nature in all their brightness and sweetness, and that in a higher degree, perhaps,

---

[238] Isaias liii. 11.
[239] 2 Cor. vi. 10.
[240] 1 Cor. iii. 23.
[241] Ps. xxiii. 1.

than the lord of the soil. The beauty of the world is a common inheritance, and none enjoy it so keenly as those who by the *donum scientiae* see God in everything, and everything in God.[242] The whole world to them is like the bush that burned on Mount Horeb. The presence and glory of God are everywhere. "All things" are theirs; and this includes the whole revelation of God, and the whole regeneration of mankind. A priest begins the day at the altar within the veil, encompassed by the Divine Presence and the heavenly court. The vision of faith, conscious and unconscious, becomes a second nature. He sees always the world that is invisible. Its beauty, its sweetness, and its fragrance are perceptible to an inward sense. The incense of the Holy Mass in the morning, and of the Benediction of the evening, is as an odour from the eternal hills. A priest whose mind is full of this world must be often, if not always, spiritless and saddened. A priest whose mind is filled with the eternal world will be always — habitually and virtually, and very often actually — filled with its light, peace, and gladness. The promise of God by the prophet is fulfilled in him: "The Lord will give thee rest continually," even in the disorders of this tumultuous world, "and will fill thy soul with brightness," *implebit splendoribus animam tuam*; the darkness without, his soul will be filled with the splendours of the world of light. "And thou shalt be like a watered garden," a garden for order and beauty, which is dressed by God Himself, and watered with continual streams: "and like a

---

[242] "Fidelis homo cujus totus mundus divitiarum est, et quasi nihil habens omnia possidet inhaerendo tibi cui serviunt omnia." — S. Aug. Confess., lib. v. i.

fountain of water, whose waters shall not fail."[243] He shall not alone receive the streams from "the Fountain of living water," which is God Himself, but he shall in himself be a fountain of perennial water, from which streams shall flow, not only into his own inward being, but outwardly upon all around him — streams of light, of charity, of consolation, and of saving health; for the sacramental grace of his priesthood and the seven gifts of the Holy Ghost will be always and everywhere, and in all needs and trials *Fons aquae salientis in vitam aeternam*.[244] This alone would be an abundant reward to the most fervent priest who had spent himself through a long life for the elect's sake. But there are also other rewards.

1. And first is the joy of a pastor over the souls of his flock. The relation of pastor and flock is threefold — mutual knowledge, mutual love, mutual charity. The mutual knowledge is to know the number, the name, and the needs of his flock one by one, and to be known by them as their father, friend, and guide: the mutual charity is that he loves them for our Lord's sake, for their own sake, as heirs of eternal life, and as his spiritual children in Jesus Christ: and the mutual service is that he bestows upon them his care, labour, time, strength, health, and, if need be, life itself; and that they render to him the service of filial charity, generosity, and obedience. When pastor and flock are so united, then the words of S. John are fulfilled: "I have no greater grace than this, to hear that my

---

[243] Isaias lviii. 11.
[244] S. John iv. 14.

children walk in truth."[245] In the measure in which the love of souls reigns in a priest's heart he will understand this joy, and his joy will be in measure equal to his love. But the love of souls is a sixth sense. Some men have so little of it as to seem to have none: some so much that it controls all their life. Some priests have, indeed, a love of souls, and yet so unconstraining and so tame that they have little joy and little recompense in their work. But to those in whom the fire is kindled there are three distinct joys, so diverse that they cannot be compared, and yet so alike that they spring from one motive.

The first is joy over the innocent— that is, over the children who as yet are fresh in their baptismal grace; still more over those who have grown up to youth, to manhood, and to womanhood with the innocence of childhood. There can be no more beautiful sight in this world than a soul in grace. In the kingdom of their Father they shall shine as the sun:[246] already in this world in the sight of God they so bear His image and likeness that its brightness is not overcast by any cloud of wilful sin. They are the clean in heart who see God, and the peacemakers who are the sons of God. The humility, purity, sincerity, and charity of such souls in all their relations in life, and not least to him who has been the guide of their youth and both father and friend in God, is to a priest the seal and sign that his work is accepted by our Divine Master.

---

[245] 3 S. John 4.
[246] S. Matt. xiii. 43

But another and distinct recompense of all cares, anxieties, and labours is to be found in the conversion of sinners and the return of souls to God. The joy of the Good Shepherd over the lost sheep will be measured by two things — the danger of the soul and the labour of the search. Sometimes one who has long persevered in innocence falls like lightning from heaven. Yesterday he was in union with God; today he is cut off and dead. All the grace of childhood and youth is gone, and the brightness is turned into death. And a dead soul, like a dead body, soon decays. One sin opens the floodgate, and the rapidity of the stream is preternatural. Once fallen, the facility is acquired, not by habit, but by a new and strange impulse unknown before. Then comes reckless continuance in sin, and then despair; and despair makes the soul blind and deaf. Every priest has had, or sooner or later will have, this sorrow; and he will remember the prayers and efforts, and hopes and disappointments, it may be of years, before the lost soul was found and brought back to God. S. Augustine gives the example of three who were dead brought back to life again. The daughter of Jairus, only just dead, before decay began: the widow's son, dead and carried out to burial, dead and under the dominion of decay: and Lazarus, dead and four days in the grave, bound by the winding-sheet and blindfold with the napkin, like the sin that is deadly, habitual, and blinding. The joy over such resurrections from the dead none can measure but the priest who has received back his "dead to life again."[247]

Lastly, there is the consolation, still full of

---

[247] Heb. xi. 35.

sadness and anxiety, when those who have fallen again and again, again and again return, and are received back once more. It is a joy with trembling. For those on whom we "have mercy in fear," "pulling them out of the fire,"[248] continue for a long time, perhaps forever, a cause of constant fear. Nevertheless, when the pastor has done all he can for them, he may rest in hope. If souls will not be redeemed he cannot save them. God Himself respects the freedom He created and gave to them. They can destroy themselves. As life draws on, and the work of a priest in the midst of his flock has brought him into contact with the good and the evil, the innocent and the penitent, he can look round upon it as the sower in the lingering summer when the corn is ripening, looks upon the harvest-field. He sees the mildew and the blight, and here and there many a stalk laid by the rain and wind, pale and sickly; but the field is full of life, and the sun is upon the reddening ears, in a little while to be reaped for the great harvest-home. And in the midst of many sorrows he can rejoice as in the joy of harvest: "*Laetabuntur coram te, sicut qui laetantur in messe*".[249]

2. Another reward of a fervent priest is the gratitude of his flock. He may say, "Therefore, my dearly beloved brethren, and most desired, my joy and my crown."[250] "If I be made a victim upon the sacrifice and service of your faith, I joy and rejoice with you all. In the self-same thing do you also joy

---

[248] S. Jude 23.
[249] Isaias ix. 3.
[250] Philip, iv. 1.

and rejoice with me."[251] "Ye have known us in part that we are your glory, even as ye also are ours in the day of our Lord Jesus Christ."[252] "For what is our hope, or joy, or crown of glory? Are not you in the presence of our Lord Jesus Christ at His coming?"[253] "Because now we live, if you stand in the Lord. For what thanks can we return to God for you, in all the joy wherewith we rejoice for you before our God?"[254] When he counts up his sheep, he may be ever saying, *Corona mea et gaudium meum*. When he numbers up the sinners and impenitent, and the wrecked homes which he has laboured to save, he will remember how he has striven and prayed, how for their salvation he has "toiled all night" in the dark, with hardly a ray of hope, "and taken nothing," ready again to let down the nets at our Lord's bidding, and again to launch out into the deep, out of which all his striving and all his prayers have not yet saved them. This must meet us, as it met our Divine Master, in our daily labour. When we look upon them, we share the mental sorrows of our Lord on earth; when from them we turn to the field white for the harvest, He gives us a share of His joy in heaven.

There are five companies among his people who reward a priest in this life. First, every penitent soul has a history full of the sin of man and the love of God. Some were all but drowned in sin, and some were plucked from the fire. We did not know them before; they were brought to us as by chance.

---

[251] Ibid. ii. 17,18.
[252] 2 Cor. i. 14.
[253] 1 Thess. ii. 19, 20.
[254] Ibid. iii. 8, 9.

They were, as they thought, avoiding our confessional when they came into it; they thought to escape from us, when unconsciously they took themselves in the snare which was laid for them, not by us, who knew nothing of them, but by the hand of God. To bring back souls to God, and to see the likeness of God once more shine out from the darkness of their past, and to watch over their steadfast perseverance in the way of life, is a recompense beyond all labours.

Next come the mourners.

S. Barnabas had a title brighter than a crown. He was *Filius Consolationis,* a son of the consolation of Israel, and a messenger of the glad tidings of good; and that because he was "full of the Holy Ghost," a disciple of the Paraclete, the Divine Comforter. A priest's ministry is twofold. He is a physician to heal both sin and sorrow: these are distinct but inseparable, and each needs a distinct treatment. Many who can deal with sin are unskilful in dealing with sorrow. To deal with sinners sometimes makes us hard, as if sorrows were imaginary. But no man can be a son of consolation who has not known sorrow for his own sin, sorrow in penance, sorrow for the sins of others, sorrow for the wreck which death has wreaked upon the world. The beatitude, "Blessed are they that mourn, for they shall be comforted," is a promise that God will console them, not only by the Paraclete, but by those who are consecrated to be "sons of consolation" — the priests and pastors who share the office, the tenderness, and the sympathies of our great High Priest, the Man of Sorrows, and the fountain of all consolation.

And after the mourners come a multitude of little children.

Among the many rewards of a faithful priest come the love and the joy of children. By the faith infused in Baptism, they recognise in the priest a spiritual fatherhood. Children come round a priest not only by a natural instinct, drawn by kindness, but by a supernatural instinct as to one who belongs to them by right. The love of children for a priest is the most unselfish love on earth, and so long as they are innocent it binds them to him by a confidence which casts out fear. The most timid and shrinking come to him as a relief and protection. They tell him everything — their hopes and fears, their troubles and their faults — with an undoubting confidence in his love and care. No priest has greater joy than the priest who loves his schools, and trains with his own eye and care the boys who surround his altar. It is one of the signs of his conformity to his Divine Master.

Next after them come the poor. A priest is God's almoner. If he has nothing of his own, he receives in alms from the hand of His Master, and he distributes it again to the poor. The old, the helpless, and the destitute turn to him as their last hope. What Job in his profound humility said no priest will dare to say; yet every true priest would desire to be said of him when he is dead: "The ear that heard me blessed me, and the eye that saw me gave witness to me. Because I had delivered the poor man that cried out, and the fatherless that had no helper, the blessing of him that was ready to perish came upon me, and I comforted the heart of the widow. I was an eye to the blind and a foot to the lame; I was the father of the poor, and the cause which I knew not I searched out diligently."[255] The poorest man ought to have no fear of coming to a priest, for a priest is not his own — he belongs to his flock, and every one has a right to him and to his service in the charity of Jesus Christ. To be loved by the poor is the surest sign a priest can have that he is not unlike his Master. For the people heard Him gladly. Their love is a great reward. When the world is dark and hostile, a priest takes sanctuary among his poor. Almost all the great in Church or State were against S. Thomas of Canterbury, but the poor priests and the poor people were always with him.

Lastly, there is a company who cannot come about the priest day by day like the others — that is, the sick and the dying. The two chief works of a pastor are the preparing of children for their warfare in life, and the preparing of the sick for the last conflict in death. The school and the sickroom are the two chief fields of a priest's charity and fervour. Sickness weighs heavily upon heart and mind. The sick are often sad and oppressed by the consciousness of sins, both of evil done and good undone, and through weakness they are unable to throw the burden off. They often say that they cannot pray, and that they cannot think: they can only lie and suffer. It is at such a time that a priest can think for them, and call their thoughts into activity. If he be a "fountain of water whose waters shall not fail," then he will refresh the soul that is dry through suffering and parched by mental

---

[255] Job xxix. 11-16.

anxiety. What is true of the sick is still more true of the dying. In the last hours the voice of a good priest is as the voice of a messenger from God — that is, of God Himself. The whispered name of Jesus, and the acts of faith, hope, charity, and contrition breathed into the ear that will soon hear no more, are the end of his pastoral care. The sanctified sufferings of the sick and the saint-like transit of the dying; the thanks of the sick and passing soul even in broken words, or by the last transient gleam of a peaceful and grateful look, are a reward beyond all earthly recompense.

When the penitents and mourners and children and the poor love and surround a priest, he has the surest countersigns of his Master's love. The special friends of Jesus are his friends, and in him they see both the servant and the Lord.

3. The last reward of a good priest is a happy death. A calm conscience in charity with all men is the witness of God's work in him. The priest may say, "Being confident of this very thing, that He who hath begun a good work in me will perfect the same until the day of Jesus Christ,"[256] *Ipse perficiet.* "We know that we have passed from death unto life because we love the brethren."[257] We not only believe and hope, but we know. We know that where there is a stream there must be a fountain. We know that the love of brotherhood flows from the love of God. Whosoever loves God is united with Him, and the second death has no power over those that are His. A good priest will say, "I am not

---

[256] Phil. i. 6.
[257] 1 S. John iii. 14.

conscious to myself of anything, yet am I not hereby justified. He that justifieth me is the Lord."[258] His sentence I await. Nevertheless, "if our heart reprehendeth us not, then we have confidence towards God."[259]

And when his hour is come there will go up from every home, and from every heart in his flock, and from many who are his spiritual children scattered abroad, a multitude of unceasing prayers. None die so happily, or surrounded by such a wide and ardent charity, as a pastor. His life has been a life of charity to penitents, to mourners, to children, to the poor, and they cannot recompense him except by their prayers, and their prayers have great power with God. They will surround his home in his last hours. And the presence of Jesus will surround his dying bed. He has lived in close and constant relation with his Divine Master for many years; and now He is come to call him to his eternal rest and to the exceeding great reward, to the glory and the crown that shall be given to him.

In the state of waiting and expiation daily prayers and Masses will be offered for him. As he has done to others so now his flock will do for him. Then comes the transit to the essential glory, which will be measured by the merit laid up in this life; but the merit is measured by charity. As he has loved God in this life so will he see God with a greater intensity in the Beatific Vision: and as he has lived in charity with all men so will be his bliss in the Communion of Saints. Add to this the accidental

---

[258] 1 Cor. iv. 4.
[259] 1 S. John iii. 21.

glory, the ever-increasing bliss and joy over sinners that repent and souls that persevere, after his death, but through the labours of his life. Though dead he yet will speak; the inheritance of his labours will live on. The memory of his name will spread, and after many days, when he is in the eternal kingdom, the first seeds cast by him will be ever springing up. The evil we do lives after us and reproduces itself: so by God's mercy does the good. The seeds scattered in the furrow, and sown beside all waters, in the morning and in the evening will bear a harvest and be reaped by other hands, but the reward will yet be his.

If such be the priest's rewards springing up in this life, and ascending into the heavenly court, with how great a love ought we to love our work. The pastoral care is to be loved everywhere, because it is the test and proof of our love to our Divine Redeemer. It is also the most perfect discipline of charity, the most searching abnegation of self, the most generous sacrifice of all things and of ourselves also for the salvation of souls. It is moreover the fullest fountain of sanctification, and as we live in the exercise of charity, so every act may have its augmentation. If the pastoral office is to be loved everywhere, it is to be loved especially in England. We are pastors of the poor, and poor ourselves, separate from courts and honours, slighted and set aside in apostolic liberty, in faith and work independent of all human authority, closely and vitally united with the See of Peter and with the Church throughout the world: heirs of the Martyrs, Saints, Confessors of every age, from S. Augustine to this day. Their names and their memories are upon the cities and fields of England.

As in the early times, when the Church at its first uprising began in the houses of the faithful, till it came forth from penal laws and hiding-places into the light of day, so has it been with us. All this binds together the pastors and people in England by a mutual dependence and with a primitive charity, on which as yet the world has not breathed its withering taint. Happy the priest who loves his pastor's lot and lives wholly in it, fulfilling day by day the slight and despised acts of charity to all who need his care, and laying up in heaven unconsciously the gold dust of a humble life, looking only for his eternal reward.

CHAPTER XVIII.

THE PRIEST'S HOUSE.

The Fourth Provincial Council of Westminster decreed as follows:

1. "Let presbyteries be the true homes of peace and of charity, of sobriety and of modesty; a notable example in all things to the faithful, 'that the adversary may have no evil to say of us.'[260] Let simplicity be their adornment; nor let anything there be found, in furniture or decoration, that ministers to luxury or to worldly desires. Let there be no ludicrous or foolish pictures, or any others unfitting the eyes of priest; but in every room let there be the crucifix, or the image of the most Holy Mother of God, or of the Saints, or pictures representing the life of our Saviour or sacred history."

The furniture of a priest's house ought to be plain and solid — plain, that is, unlike the fanciful and costly furniture of domestic houses; and solid, because it ought to last for generations of priests succeeding one another. As far as possible it ought to be alike in all rooms. Equality is a part of brotherly charity. S. Paul warns the Corinthians, who had "houses to eat and drink in," not to "put to shame those who had none."[261] If one priest has money and another has none, it is a part of charity in the richer to be as the poorer in all such accidents

---

[260] S. Tit. ii. 8.
[261] 1 Cor. xi. 22.

as furniture and the like. Contrasts are wounding, and a temptation to those who have money.

The exclusion of foolish and unseemly pictures needs no comment. The presence everywhere of the crucifix and sacred pictures is most wholesome as a mental discipline for ourselves, and as a silent witness to the world. A priest's house cannot be like the house of a layman without our seeming at least to be ashamed of our Master.

The Council of Carthage says: "Let the Bishop have furniture, table, and food cheap and poor, and let him seek the authority of his dignity in the merit of his faith and life."[262] If this be so for Bishops, then also for priests.

2. "Let regularity be observed in all things. Let the priest say Mass at the hour fixed. And though he ought to be always ready to hear confessions, let him be found especially punctual in the confessional, or at least in the church, on the appointed days and hours, lest, from want of order and method, there arise scandal and injury to souls. Keep order, and order will keep you."

Want of punctuality, especially on weekdays, is a common fault, and a constant complaint from the faithful, above all from men in professions or in commerce, who are either deprived thereby of Mass, or involved in serious damage. The loss of souls through irregular attendance in the confessional, or refusing to hear a confession out of hours, or at dinner-time, or recreation, or supper-

---

[262] Conc. Carthag. See Conc. Trid. sess. xxv. c. i. De Ref.

time, will never be known in this world. We ought to be afraid of failing to hear a confession when asked, unless we know by previous and certain knowledge that there is no need. But who can be sure of this?

3. "Let no women reside in the priest's house without leave of the Ordinary. Schoolmistresses and their pupil-teachers, as being more refined in intelligence and character, and therefore more exposed to the tongues of calumniators, are altogether forbidden ever to reside in the presbytery with the clergy, unless for some reason known to the Bishop, and approved by him in writing. 'Let the servants who attend on the priests be of an advanced age, modest, prudent, and of a blameless life, ascertained by experience, that the injunctions of the Canons be obeyed.'[263] Therefore let priests by all means beware of certain women, who, by domineering and despising the poor of Christ, and sowing discords by whispering, become truly the pests of the mission. Furthermore, we forbid the clergy to allow the schoolmistresses or their pupil-teachers, or the women-servants of the house, to sit at table with them."

This paragraph would be obscured by any comment.

4. "Let no priest reside in a hired or private house without the previous consent of the Bishop."[264]

---

[263] I. Conc. Westm. Dec. xxiv. 4.
[264] Synod. Thurles. *De Vita et Hon. Clericorum*, n. 16, p. 33.

5. "Whosoever is set over a church, whether he be simple missionary, or be entitled missionary rector, is held to be the steward of God, to whom is intrusted a part of the Lord's vineyard. Let him, therefore, be useful and faithful, in everything laborious, remembering that the safety or the danger of the commander of the ship and of those who are on board is the same. Where, then, there are two or more priests in a mission, let one only, independently of all except the Ordinary, exercise the office committed to him, and all others dependently from him. The assistant priests receive faculties from the Bishop; but to preserve order we enjoin them that they do not use those faculties except under the government of the rector of the church, for which cause let the following or like words be inserted in the formula of faculties: 'In dependence on the rector of the church to which you are attached.'" [265] The head priest of each church has the sole stewardship and administration. He depends only on the Bishop, and his assistants depend on him. This is expressed in the faculties held by each. To the head priests, therefore, belongs the decision of every question; and the Council orders and commands *(praecipimus)* the assistant priests to use even their faculties in dependence — that is, obedience — to him.

6. "To the rector or head priest are intrusted the church and people, the schools and presbytery, all goods of the mission, and, lastly, even the clergy who serve the church; therefore the account of all these is to be rendered to the Bishop by him alone and exclusively. Further, by law or custom, all

---

[265] I. Conc. Westm. Dec. xxv.

rectors and their assistants are wont to inhabit the same presbytery; but the presbytery is the house of the rector so long as he discharges the office of rector and holds the diocesan faculties. To him alone belongs the right of administering and ruling the same; neither is it a right only, but an obligation; 'but if any man knows not how to rule his own house, how shall he take care of the Church of God?'[266] Let him know of what spirit he is himself, and how among priests mutual charity and reverence of heart ought constantly to be seen from one to another. Let him, therefore, be as the elder among his assistants, not as lording it over the clergy, but as their father, or rather as their eldest brother. For they ought to be trained and taught as the servants of the Good Shepherd, who in their time shall themselves be worthy and capable of ruling missions. Moreover, from the fact that the cure of souls is committed in chief to the rectors of the missions, the assistants must not think that they are free from so great a burden; for it is their part in dependence on the rector to help him, that is, in preaching, in hearing confessions, in teaching Catechism to children, in visiting the sick, and in administering to them the Sacraments, and in fulfilling the other offices of missionaries."

In this paragraph are laid down the following principles:

(1) That the rector or head priest is trustee of the whole mission, church, people, school, presbytery, goods, and clergy. The last is the only point we need now to notice. The rector is

---

[266] 1 S, Tim. iii. 5.

responsible for his brother priests, for their personal, priestly, and pastoral life. He is answerable to the Bishop for them. And they are bound to recognise that responsibility. As they bear themselves to him, so some day their assistants will bear themselves in turn to them.

(2) That they ought all to live together under one roof. Priests dwelling alone are in an abnormal, unecclesiastical, unsacerdotal state, which often has grave dangers, and is never free from many disadvantages. The liberty of living alone is not wholesome; and the loss of the daily discipline of self-abnegation in living with others is a privation of much good.

(3) That the rector is bound by the highest obligations of charity and consideration towards those under him, and they also are bound by the duty of obedience, brotherly love, and mutual respect as king's sons to each other, and above all to him.

(4) That a presbytery ought to be a pastoral seminary, to keep alive the training of their youth, and to perfect it in the maturity of their manhood and of their priesthood, that they also may one day, as elders and superiors, train and teach the young priests who shall be intrusted to them.

(5) That, though the rector has the cure of souls in chief, they also are responsible, but in dependence on the rector, for all the work, for all the failures, and for all the omissions of work in the mission.

7. "The *mensa* or common table in a presbytery is the token and pledge of brotherly charity, which is lessened by absence. If absence happens often, it altogether undoes charity. Therefore let them seldom go abroad to the tables of others, much less let them frequent them; having food and wherewith to be covered, with these we are content."[267]

In the measure in which we have brotherly charity we shall understand the meaning and the power of the *mensa communis*. In the measure in which we disregard the admonitions of the common table we may suspect, or rather we may be sure, that our brotherly love is low in fervour and dim of sight. The wholesome equality of Christian brotherhood is recognised and sustained by the contentment and abnegation of self, by which they who have money, or rich relations, or many friends, deny themselves for the sake of those who have not. It is a danger to a priest to have many "houses to eat and drink in," and it is a grace to others to have none.

Those mission-houses are the happiest in which all things are, as far as possible, in common, where each is content with his *honorarium*, and his share of the Easter offerings, and of all oblations thrown into one sum, so as to exclude the unwise partialities of the people, and sometimes the temptations of priests.

8. "It is to be desired that the common recreation of priests should be made, as a rule, one

---

[267] 1 S. Tim. vi. 8.

with another at home rather than abroad. 'How good and how pleasant it is that brethren dwell in unity.' For to be present at the recreation in common confirms and strengthens charity, and gives day by day occasions of exercising it in word and deed."

Men are hardly known until they unbend themselves. Official relations are distant and artificial. In recreation the man comes out through the priest. There is no greater or surer test of humility, charity, and human kindliness. Pride, haughty manners, high looks, fastidiousness, contempt of what they think below them, criticism, and the habit of slighting inferiors in birth, culture, or refinement, are detected as by a chemical test in recreation — that is, in the easy talk at the common table or after it. Recreation is the pillory of pride. It proclaims the offender, and holds him up to be pelted.

9. "Let priests abstain from exhibitions unworthy of ecclesiastics, from the clamours of hunting with horse and hounds, from public dancing and unlawful games, and from feastings which are protracted to unseasonable hours of night." [268] "We strictly forbid, moreover, all ecclesiastics in sacred Orders to be present at scenic representations in public theatres, or in places which serve for the time as a public theatre, imposing upon the transgressors the pain of suspension incurred thereby ipso facto, hitherto in force in England, and reserved to the Ordinaries respectively."

---

[268] Conc. Westm. Dec. xxiv. 1.

May this wise and wholesome tradition of our forefathers never be relaxed. The theatre in their days was high, intellectual, and pure compared with the modern stage and its moral fall.

In his epistle to Donatus, S. Cyprian denounces theatres: *poenitenda contagia…Adulterium discitur dum videtur, et lenocinante ad vitia publicae auctoritatis malo*[269] S. John Chrysostom calls fathers who took their sons to theatres παιδοχτονουσ.[270] But we may be told that this refers to the heathen stage. In the year 1596 the Council of Aquileia decreed: *Ad spectacula comaediorum, sive ad bancos circulatorum et bufforum in plateis, qui alias exemplum esse debent maturitatis et prudentiae accedere et assistere clericos non decet.*[271] The Council of Trent decrees as follows: "The Holy Synod ordains that those things which at other times have been decreed by Pontiffs and sacred Councils concerning the life, the dignity, the cultivation, the instruction of clerics are to be retained; as also the decrees concerning gaming, feasting, dances, dice, and sports and offences of all kinds; also as to the avoiding of secular business."[272]

10. "Having before our eyes the golden axiom of the sacerdotal life given by the Apostle, 'All things are lawful to me, but all things are not expedient;'[273] and again, 'All things are lawful to

---

[269] S. Cypr. Ep. i. p. 4, ed. Rigalt.
[270] Homily against Games and Theatres, Opp. tom. vi. p. 274.
[271] Conc. Aquil. cap. xi.
[272] Sess. xxii. c. i.
[273] 1 Cor. vi. 12.

me, but all things do not edify:'[274] let priests direct all things to the good of others, and to the gaining of greater graces. Let them not too easily or too often go to places of public concourse and recreation, even though they be reputable, lest by wasting time they be suspected of an unsacerdotal spirit. Unless for duties of necessity or charity, let them return early at nightfall to the presbytery. To abstain from unlawful things is little, unless, being zealous for the better gifts, we know how to use lawful things sparingly and to edification. [275] We therefore lovingly in the Lord beseech our beloved clergy to observe the aforesaid prohibitions not only in the letter, but also in the spirit, interpreting them with piety."

On these *minora moralia* little comment can be made without weakening their searching force. There is only one point which may be noted. We are exhorted to observe these prohibitions *secundum spiritum* — as those who are even now being judged before your Divine Master by the "law of liberty;" and not this only, but *pie interpretantes,* reading their inmost meaning with a loving desire to fulfil, and even if we can to go beyond, what they literally require. The slothful servant and the mistrustful, the grudging and the cold-hearted, go by the letter, and search for probable opinions to evade the letter, *littera occidet.* And thus our generous Master is ungenerously served.

---

[274] Ibid. x. 23.
[275] "*Habent sancti viri hoc proprium ut quo semper ab illicitis longe sint a se plerumque etiam licita abscindant.*" — S. Greg. M, *Dialog*, lib. iv. c. xi.

11. "A hard and morose spirit is unbecoming in a priest who labours in the midst of the people; a modest cheerfulness, if only in season, is not to be reproved, but is worthy of praise. We praise therefore those missionaries who, following the example of Saints, strive to draw the youth committed to their charge from dangerous representations by innocent recreations. In doing which let them always take care to refresh and not to relax their minds; and while they give pleasure to others not to hurt themselves. Which is at once to be observed in treating of sodalities of women. Let the priest as far as possible preside over their recreations by other women rather than in person, lest he give a handle to the tongues of detractors. But let priests suppress the abuse which has grown up in some places of holding balls to raise money for the schools and other pious works.

"As to the public recreations which are called excursions, we have with sorrow heard very many evils thence resulting. We judge therefore that they are rather to be repressed than promoted. However, lest we should seem to be hard in matters lawful in themselves, we exhort the pastors of souls to abstain from promoting excursions unless they have leave for them from the Vicar-General."

12. "The dress of ecclesiastics ought to be such as to distinguish them altogether from laymen, and yet not to confound them with heterodox ministers. Let it, therefore, be of a black or dark colour; and let them never, under the pretext of travelling, return to the ignominy of the secular dress, from which they have been set free. We

commend the kind of dress which, a few years ago, the secular clergy began to wear. At home, however, it is above all fitting that they should wear the cassock, or, if they will, what is called the *zimarra* and biretta.

"But inasmuch as the peculiar (proper) mark of the Catholic clergy in all the world is what is commonly called the Roman collar, which already among us is recognised as such by Protestants, without provoking contumely or offence, we will that all priests should wear it in the exercise of their sacred ministry, unless, perchance, for a time, at the discretion of the Bishops, by reason of circumstances, it be otherwise ordered."

13. "To these decrees, this Fourth Synod judges it expedient in the Lord that certain additions be made. We order, therefore, that every priest shall wear the Roman collar not only when he exercises the sacred ministry, but at all times, so that he may be known by all to be a priest. We decree also that the usage of Rome be observed by all ecclesiastics — that is, of not wearing the hair either on the cheeks nor as a beard."

14. "And if any priest shall wear the clerical dress so changed — save in the rarest case to be approved by the Ordinary— that he cannot be known by all to be a priest belonging to the clergy of this Province, or so as to fall under the suspicion of the faithful or notoriously to give them scandal, let them not be admitted to say Mass, nor in assisting at the divine offices, into the sanctuary."

15. "Our forefathers, assembled in the

Council of London in the year 1248, declared that to put off the clerical dress is a very grave and wanton abuse, by which God is said to be mocked, the honour of the Church obscured, the dignity of the clerical order degraded; Christ, when His soldiers wear other uniforms, is deserted; the honour and dignity of the Church is stained when the beholder cannot distinguish a cleric from a laic at a glance, and so the priest becomes a scandal and despised by all who are truly faithful."

16. "The Bishop of Chalcedon, the second Ordinary for England and Scotland after the overthrow of the Hierarchy in these kingdoms, exhorted our predecessors, the companions of martyrs, and themselves true confessors for the faith, in these words:

'Let missionaries be content with the food set before them. Let them ask for nothing unusual unless health requires it. In their dress let them wear nothing which savours of vanity or expense; let them abstain from loud laughing, and from every gesture of body which savours of levity; knowing of a certainty, as Ecclesiasticus says, that the clothing of the body, and the laughter of the teeth, and the gait of a man tell what he is.

'Let them avoid idleness as the surest root of temptations to evil; and for that cause let them have with them at least the sacred Scriptures, on which let them perpetually meditate.

'Let them not contend with any priest, above all with their elders, to whom let them show all reverence and honour, that by their example they may show the laity how they should bear themselves towards priests.

'Let them beware of the habit of objecting or of opposing themselves to what others say, as they used in the schools by way of exercise, because in the familiar intercourse among men it is highly odious.

'Let them not easily believe any ill of their fellow priests and brethren, nor by any means publish it, or lend an ear to those who do so."'

On all this wise and weighty teaching, so high in aspiration and so minute in direction, only one word need be said. Good will it be for us if we, too, have at least the sacred Scripture and perpetually meditate upon it. S. Charles called the Holy Scripture the Bishop's garden. Few walk in it, and fewer dress it. And for that cause so much of the word of man, and so little of the Word of God, is preached to the people. S. Teresa said that one chief cause of the evils of her day was ignorance of the Holy Scripture. "Sal etenim terrae non sumus si corda audientium non condimus. Quia dum nos ab orationis et eruditionis sanctae usu cessamus sal infatuatum est."[276] By whose fault is this, but of priests who do not study, and therefore do not teach, the Word of God to the people? Have we not reason to ask, "Lord, is it I?"

---

[276] S. Greg. M. in Evang. tom. i. pp. 1396-1399.

CHAPTER XIX.

THE PRIEST'S LIFE.

The Fourth Provincial Council has also traced out in its twelfth decree what a priest's life ought to be in the following words:

1. "They who are not holy ought not to lay hands on holy things.'[277] All the faithful of Christ, as the Apostle testifies, are called to be Saints.[278] But priests ought to ascend to the perfection of sanctity. 'For he who, by the necessity of his position, is compelled to teach the highest things, by the same necessity is bound to show them forth in himself.'[279] The warning is altogether fearful: 'No man ought rashly to offer himself to others as a guide in the divine light who, in all his state and habit, is not most like to God.'[280] 'For they who are appointed to divine ministries attain to a royal dignity, and ought to be perfect in virtue.'[281] For so we are taught by the Catholic Church in its solemn ritual, and in the very act of conferring the priesthood. As God commanded Moses 'to choose out seventy men from the whole people to be his helpers, to whom the Holy Ghost should distribute His gifts,' so the Lord Jesus chose out presbyters of the second order to help the Apostles — that is, the Catholic Bishops — that He might teach His Church, both by word

---

[277] Conc. Carthag.

[278] 1 Cor. i. 2.

[279] S. Greg. Cura Past. P. ii. c. iii

[280] *De Eccl. Hier.* c. v.

[281] S. Thom, lib, iv. Sent. Suppl. ad B. i. quest. xi.

and deed, that the ministers of His Church ought to be perfect in faith and in works — that is, founded in the virtue of the twofold love of God and our neighbour.'[282] For priests are chosen by God, that, being commended by heavenly wisdom, pure morals, and a lasting observance of justice, and keeping the ten commandments of the law they may be, by the Sevenfold Spirit, upright and mature in knowledge and in action; and that, preserving in their morals the integrity of a chaste and holy life, the pattern of all justice may shine forth in them.'[283]

2. "Let priests, therefore, bear in mind that sanctity in them is presupposed. 'That for the reception of sacred Orders simple sanctifying grace by no means suffices; but that beyond this, interior perfection is required, as is proved by the unanimous consent of fathers and doctors, who with one mouth demand it.'[284] No degree, therefore, of sanctity is judged to be proportionate to sacerdotal perfection[285] by the Church of God, and by God, the author of the priesthood, but that which bears some likeness of the great High Priest Jesus Christ our Lord. For the priest is set in the sight of the world, to be a living image of the life of Jesus toiling in solitude and in the straits of poverty, and suffering also the contradictions of men."

This teaches us three things: first, that interior perfection is required before ordination and as a prerequisite condition to sacred Orders;

---

[282] Pontif. Rom. in Ordin. Presbyteri.
[283] Ibid.
[284] S. Alphon *Theol. Moral, de Sacr. Ord.* lib. vi. 57.
[285] S. Greg. Naz. Orat. ii. lxvii.

secondly, that the state of the priesthood is the state of perfection; thirdly that a priest is bound to sustain himself in that state and to persevere in it to the end of life.

The perfection of man is defined by S. Bernard in these words: *Haec hominis est perfectio similitudo Dei.* But God is charity. Therefore, perfection consists essentially in this *gemina Dei et proximi dilectione.* The essential perfection is a quality of the person. The state in which a person is placed is the instrumental perfection.

The perfection of charity is determined by its extension.

The first extension is to persons, as to friends and to enemies. The second extension is to acts — that is, to the fulfilment of the commandments and of the counsels.

But the new commandment, which is twofold, includes all commandments and all counsels.

This personal perfection does not mean a sinless state, and it is compatible with infirmity and the failures of infirmity in which there is no deliberate will to sin.

S. Bernard says: *Indefessum proficiendi studium, et jugis conatus ad perfectionem perfectio reputatur.*

Studere perfectioni, esse perfectum est; profecto nolle

proficere deficere est.[286]

Such, then, is the nature of perfection to which all are called. And to this, before ordination, as the Council teaches, all who desire to enter the priesthood ought to have attained.

3. "For which reason the dignity of the priesthood is derived from a twofold source. Priests are the beloved companions of Jesus, and receive a share in His own mission, which He received of the Father. 'As the Father hath sent Me, I also send you.'[287] For they are partakers of the priesthood of Christ, and share in the twofold jurisdiction over His natural and over His mystical Body. By sacred Orders they are deputed 'to the highest ministries, by which service is rendered to Christ Himself in the Sacrament of the Altar: for which service greater interior sanctity is required than is required even by the state of religion.'[288] Moreover, they are friends, to whom He said, with familiar love, 'I will not now call you servants, but My friends, because you have known all things which I have done in the midst of you.'[289] And forasmuch as in the dispensation of redeeming grace it is so ordered that the servants of God receive the help of the Holy Ghost, according to the height of their dignity or the arduous greatness of their office, to none assuredly are given more abundant graces than to the friends and partakers of the priesthood and mission of Jesus our Saviour."

---

[286] Ep. ccliv. tom. i. p. 534.
[287] S. John XX. 21.
[288] S. Thom. Summa Theol. 2da 2dae, q. 184, a. 8.
[289] Pontif. Rom. § 1.

We have seen what sanctity is required by the manifold relations in which a priest stands to the Person of his Divine Master. Here S. Thomas tells us that it is the greatest interior sanctity required by any state on earth. And as this sanctity is required by the state itself, so it is certain that the grace and help of the Holy Ghost are always proportionate and always present for our assistance. We are always telling the people of the world that if they ever fail it is not God that fails them, but they that fail themselves; that they have always and everywhere the grace needed by their state in all straits and dangers. How much more justly and truly may they return this counsel to us if we priests fail. We are set forth first to be the pattern of the all-sufficiency of sovereign grace. Therefore, a priest is inexcusable who seeks the cause of his imperfection anywhere but in himself.

4. "How great a love of God and of souls ought, therefore, to be kindled within us, and with what a fire ought our hearts to burn. 'The flame of the pastor,' S. Bernard says, 'is the light of the flock.' For in the priest the Sacred Heart of Jesus, the principle and fountain of love and fervour, ought to live and reign. Our missionaries, kindled with the ardour of zeal for souls, will strive to deliver, by a true exposition to the people committed to them, the commandment of God, 'exceeding broad' in all fulness and sanctity. Let them take heed lest, putting darkness for light, they think it enough if they keep the faithful of Christ from mortal sin."

S. Paul tells all Christians that they are dead,

and their life hid with Christ in God.[290] He bids them, therefore, to be heavenly-minded. He bids them also to be perfect;[291] to forget the things that are behind, and to stretch forth to the things that are before, for the prize of their high vocation. S. Jude says: "But you, my beloved, building yourselves upon your most holy faith, praying in the Holy Ghost, keep yourselves in the love of God."[292] S. Paul, again, tells the Ephesians "that he prays that by comprehending with all the Saints what is the breadth, and length, and height, and depth of the love of Christ, they may be filled unto all the fulness of God." [293] And with all this before us, we hear it said that perfection is for priests, nuns, and recluses; but for all others it is lawful and enough if we aim at keeping them out of mortal sin. Few will say this; but many act as if they would say it, and as if it were their belief. Of how much glory God is robbed; of how much sanctity souls are deprived; for what innumerable venial sins they who so act are responsible; how many, walking on the boundary-line, may pass from venial to mortal sin, and therefore by low guidance how many souls may be lost.

The Provincial Council, therefore, goes on to teach as follows:

5. "Forasmuch as the distributions of the Holy Ghost are manifold and inscrutable, and as the faithful are called, some before others, to various

---

[290] Col. iii. 1.
[291] 2 Cor. xiii. 11.
[292] S. Jude 20, 21.
[293] Ephes. iii. 18,19.

degrees of perfection, it is not enough that a priest should be able to distinguish scientifically between leprosy and leprosy if he cannot discern also between spirit and spirit, lest, giving ear to the human spirit or even to the diabolical as if to the Spirit of God, he be led into error and lead others into error with him. For sometimes not only the faithful of a more cultivated intelligence, but the rude and the simple among the people, are called to the highest perfection of sanctity. Therefore the guide of souls ought so to discern and know the ascents of the heart to God and the degrees of prayer by science at least, if not by his own experience, that he may be able to confirm beginners in the purgative way, direct those who are advancing in the illuminative way, and lead upward the more perfect to higher things in the way of union. *Labia enim sacerdotis custodient scientiam, et legem requirent ex ore ejus, quia angelus Domini exercituum est.*[294] In every flock some will be found who, being called by God to the life of counsels, seek the science of the spiritual life from the lips of the priest. Let us, therefore, give all heed, lest in the hidden life of God the sheep be found going before the shepherds."

The Auctor Incertus says: "It is truly great confusion for priests and all clerics, when laymen are found more faithful and more just than they: how can it not be confusion to them to be inferior to laymen, to whom it is great confusion even to be

---

[294] Mal. ii. 7. S. Jerome says: "Si sacerdos est sciat legem: si ignorat legem ipse se arguit non esse Domini sacerdotem." — In Aggaeum.

only equal."[295] S. Ambrose says: "Vides divisiones? Nihil in sacerdotibus plebium requiri, nihil populare, nihil commune cum studio atque usu et moribus multitudinis. Sobriam a turbis gravitatem, seriam vitam, singulare pondus, dignitas sibi vindicat sacerdotalis. Quo modo enim potest observari a populo, qui nihil habet secretum a populo? dispar a multitudine? Quid enim in te miretur, si sua in te recognoscat? Si nihil in te adspiciat, quod ultra se inveniat? Si quae in se erubescit, in te quem reverendum arbitratur offendat? Supergrediamur igitur plebeias opiniones, . . . ac detritae vise orbitas declinemus."[296] In the Old Law every priest during the service of his course in the Tabernacle was forbidden to drink wine or strong drink.[297] What self-denial befits the priests of the New Law, who have no alternation of courses: they are always not only in the Tabernacle, but in the sanctuary, before the mercy seat of the Divine Presence.

The aspiration of the people for higher ways is one of the greatest rewards of a priest's life. A fervent people implies a fervent pastor. S. Bernard says truly, *Flamma pastoris lux gregis*. When the priest is kindled with the fire of the Sacred Heart his people too will walk in a great light. They will see and aspire after the higher ways of the kingdom of God. Then he will be to them *angelus Domini exercituum* — a guard and a guide.

---

[295] Auctor Operis Imperfecti inter Opp. Sti. Joan. Chrys. Hom. vi.
[296] S. Ambros. Classis i. Epist. xxviii. 2,3.
[297] Levit. x. 9.

6. "It is truly a wonderful saying of the Apostle: 'For Christ sent me not to baptise, but to preach the Gospel.'[298] Therefore in the Council of Trent we read that the chief office of Bishops is to make known the Word of God to men. That which is chief in Bishops must be surely of the highest moment for all. But as the simple and masculine preaching of the Gospel is the salvation of the hearers, so a vain and inflated declamation is to the faithful scandal, and to the preacher destruction. The mysteries of the kingdom of God are not to be handled as rhetorical exercises or lucubrations of literary art. The witness of the Holy Ghost does not need the persuasive words of man's wisdom; rather the simplicity of divine truth contemns and rejects the loftiness of our speech, that our faith may not be in the wisdom of man, but in the power of God.[299] Let all guides of souls, therefore, labour diligently, that in handling the mysteries of faith and in exhorting the faithful to piety they admit nothing that is not full of simplicity and gravity."

7. "The life of a priest is, in truth, arduous; yet it is surrounded and guarded by innumerable means and helps to acquire perfection. For our provident Mother the Church, in imposing upon the clergy the office of divine praise, vindicates and secures for its ministers in the midst of their labours of charity a time of quiet. Seven times a day it bids us ascend in heart and mind to the King of Saints and to the heavenly court; and if by the Communion of the Body and Blood of Jesus once received men may be made Saints, nothing can be

---

[298] 1 Cor. i. 17.
[299] Sess. xiv.

wanting to the companions and priests and friends of Jesus that they be made and be Saints, who are refreshed by the daily oblation of the Holy Mass and the participation of His most holy Body and Blood. All things in the priest's life contribute to this — the daily meditation on divine things; the intimate service of the most Holy Sacrament; sacred studies hardly interrupted; the ministries of charity, which, while they exhaust strength, refresh the mind; the habit also of religion and of dignity; the sign of a kingdom and of perfection which was put upon them when they were tonsured."

8. "Furthermore, to us in England in warfare for the kingdom of truth singular helps for the acquiring of sacerdotal perfection are granted by our Lord, who pities our infirmities. To the priesthood, with which missionaries are invested, the cure of souls is intrusted, and therefore all kinds of spiritual gifts which are annexed to the state of pastors; moreover, they are pastors especially of the poor, the friends of Jesus, 'who have not wherewith to recompense us,' and are poor themselves, fed and content with the alms of the poor. Add to this also the daily and almost perpetual abnegation of their own will, in bearing the burdens of others, in consoling the sick, in supporting the dying by day and by night. Finally, there remains the signal grace and privilege of the missionary oath, whereby, on the threshold of the apostolate which they have received, after the likeness of the oblation of Jesus upon the Cross, they freely offered themselves a living, daily, and acceptable sacrifice to God the Father."

The Fourth Provincial Council warns us that

we are bound to our flock by *multiplici et conscientiae et cordis ligamine* — by manifold bonds of conscience and of heart.

First, it says, "a missionary priest receives the oblations of the faithful for no other reason than because he is a missionary;" therefore he is bound to serve them. "Missionary priests are bound to labour without weariness for the salvation of the souls of those subject to their care. Let them call to mind the solemn hour in which, when invested with the ineffable dignity of priesthood, kneeling before the Bishop, they promised obedience and reverence to the Ordinary. When, therefore, they are chosen out and sent by the Bishop, to whose precepts they subjected themselves with a willing mind to fulfil the pastoral office over the sheep intrusted to him, it is plain that they are under grave obligations by the precept of obedience to fulfil rightly so great a duty.

"Moreover, by the grace of the Apostolic See three hundred years ago, it was ordained that the missionary priests in England, robbed of all maintenance by sacrilegious hands, might be admitted to sacred Orders on the title of mission, taking at the same time a truly apostolic oath for the good of the universal Church — *in bonum universalis Ecclesiae* (which Alexander VII, in the Brief *Cum circa juramenti vinculum,* on the 20th of July 1660, explained with the required declarations) — so that they might bind themselves for ever, so far as in them lay, to seek and to save the sheep of the English nation. From that most constraining bond, when a cruel persecution raged for so many years, arose and was strengthened that wonderful constancy and patience even unto martyrdom which is the crown and the glory of our clergy. Wherefore the Holy See, which still grants to the Bishops of England the faculty of ordaining their subjects on the title aforesaid, exhorts our missionaries that year by year they remember to renew the oath they have made on its anniversary (granting to them also a plenary Indulgence), and that they seriously meditate how great is the divine goodness shown to them in making them ministers of the Word to declare the wonders of His might and power; how imperishable a crown is prepared for them in heaven if they fulfil their duty in holiness; and on the contrary how strict a judgment awaits them if by their negligence or indolence, which God forbid, it happens that any perish.

"Finally, from all these (obligations) taken together — that is, from equity, from sacerdotal charity, from the promise of obedience, from the sanctity of the oath — there arises the reciprocal obligation between the priest and his own Bishop, by which both are happily bound faithfully to fulfil their respective offices, united together by common toil and by mutual co-operation."[300]

9. "Wherefore, if, which God avert, it ever happen that any one fall from the manifold grace of this state, let him know that those things which in others are light in priests ought to be judged as grave. For the most part, that which in a layman is not a fault to those in sacred Order is a sin."

A blot upon a layman's coat is little seen; a spot upon an alb cannot be hid.

---

[300] Conc. Prov. IV. Dec. x., 3-7.

The Church must guard the souls of the faithful, and the sanctity of the priesthood, and the honour of the faith, the Church and our Divine Master.

If this seems a harsh note to end with, let us remember how our Lord ended His last words before He was betrayed. He prayed for those whom He had just ordained as priests. "And now I am not in the world; and these are in the world, and I come to Thee." "Those whom Thou gavest Me I have kept, and none of them is lost but the son of perdition."[301] There will ever be wheat and tares growing together till the harvest both in the world and in the sanctuary.

CHAPTER XX.

THE PRIEST'S DEATH.

Sooner or later — soon at latest, for the longest life is short and fleet in ending — it will go abroad that we are dying. Our turn will be come. We who have lived to stand by and see so many die, as if we should live forever, we shall be lying on our deathbed at last. Will that day come upon us unawares? And shall we have time for the last Sacraments? Priests often die without them. When our people are sick, however suddenly, we are always near to watch beside them; when we are sick there is not always a priest at hand. Many priests

---

[301] S. John xvii. 11,12.

live alone, scattered at great distances from their brethren. Moreover, priests grow so familiar with death that they are often not alarmed soon enough, or they are unconscious of their danger. It seems strange that a priest who so long has been preparing others to die should need it himself. Sometimes he is too hopeful, sometimes he procrastinates, and what is often said is often true — he dies without the last Sacraments.

Some men do not like talking about death. Nobody dies of it. But it is ominous to some minds, like a winding-sheet in the candle, or the death-watch. They do not really believe these things, nevertheless they feel an unreasonable awe. They shrink from making their will. They have it in their room ready for signature. They put off signing it to to-morrow and to the next day, and at last they bequeath loss to the Church and trouble to everybody by dying intestate. Such are the freaks of the human spirit. A good man will not so fear death, and a wise man will often speak of it. Joseph of Arimathaea made his tomb in his garden, where he saw it day by day. S. Charles talked of his death continually. If we did so it would become a familiar and kindly thought, like rest after toil, and home after peril by land or by sea. We should be kept by the fear of death from resisting or grieving the Holy Ghost by any willing acts of variance with His will, and we should be trained by the thought of death to understand the words, *Cupio dissolvi et esse cum Christo.*[302] *Mihi vivere Christus, mori lucrum.*[303] *Scio enim, cui credidi, et certus sum, quia potens est depositum meum*

---

[302] Philip, i. 23.
[303] ibid. i. 21.

servare in illum diem.[304]

We are always saying, *A subitanea et improvisa morte libera nos Domine,* and no men have greater need; for our familiarity with death deadens the awfulness of the sight, and we may cease both to fear death and to prepare for it. It is to pastors especially that the words are spoken. To some: "I know thy works and thy labour and thy patience, and how thou canst not bear them that are evil." "But I have somewhat against thee, because thou hast left thy first charity. Be mindful, therefore, from whence thou art fallen, and do penance, and do the first works. Or else I come to thee, and will move thy candlestick out of its place, except thou do penance."[305] Again: "I know thy works, that thou hast the name of being alive, and thou art dead. Be watchful, and strengthen the things that remain that are ready to die, for I find not thy works full before my God." "If, then, thou shalt not watch, I will come to thee as a thief, and thou shalt not know at what hour I will come to thee."[306] And to many more among us these words are spoken: "I know thy works, that thou art neither cold nor hot. I would thou wert cold or hot. But because thou art lukewarm, and neither cold nor hot, I will begin to vomit thee out of My mouth." And to how many of us who are at ease in self-complacency the Divine Voice is ever saying, and often in vain, "Because thou sayest, I am rich and made wealthy, and have need of nothing, and knowest not that thou art wretched and miserable and poor and blind and

---

[304] 2 S. Tim, i. 12.
[305] Apoc. ii. 2, 4, 5.
[306] Ibid. iii. 1-3.

naked, I counsel thee to buy of Me gold fire-tried, that thou mayst be made rich, and mayst be clothed in white garments, and that the shame of thy nakedness may not appear; and anoint thy eyes with eye-salve, that thou mayst see." If the sadder death-beds here supposed be many, it is because they are of many kinds. All deaths of the penitent and the fervent are good: and one example is enough.

1. First, there is the death of a sinful priest; perhaps without the last Sacraments, as of an outcast, from whom it justly takes that which he seemeth to have; or, perhaps, and more fearful still, with the last Sacraments, but received in sacrilege. Next to the immutable malice of Satan is the hardness of an impenitent priest. Priests who fall, if they do not return to God with greater facility and speed than other men, may become blinder and more hardened in heart than all other sinners.[307] They have been so long familiar with all the eternal truths, they have preached them so often, they have handled all the holy things of the sanctuary, they have had so great a profusion of lights, warnings, and calls to repentance, they have had a *gratia status* so abundant, and all in vain, that their end is like the dying man, on whom all remedies, medicines, and skill have been exhausted, but death has fastened so firmly that the dying must surely die.

---

[307] "Quis unquam vidit clericum cito poenitentiam agentem?" — Auctor Incert. in Matthaeum, Hom. xl. tom. vi. p. 167.

"Laici delinquentes facile emendantur, clerici autem si semel mali evaserint inemendabiles fiunt." — S. Bonav. *Pharetrae,* lib. i. c. xxii.

How often he has preached truths which have converted and sanctified the humble, the clean in heart, the pure in life. But it was the dead preaching to the living. How often he has said Mass with a threefold sacrilege — in consecrating, in communicating to himself, in communicating to others. It was a life written within and without with judgment against himself, and a life of unworthy handling of holy things. *Sancta non sancte sed perverse, turpiter, et ad mortem.* Then comes the end. A brother priest stands by him; but what is the soul within him? Is there a pulse of life, a beat of the heart, a ray of self-knowledge, a will to repent? Perhaps he was once an innocent boy, a youth of many hopes, a quick learner, a promising seminarist, a priest full of early aspirations and sincere intentions and good resolutions. But there was a flaw in the heart — some sin of the flesh or of the spirit, some passion or some pride. It was, perhaps, known and resisted, long kept down; in an evil hour of opportunity, facility, fascination, weakness, and strong temptation the lurking enemy mastered his will, and the priest became a slave. Many years ran on; many falls, returns, and relapses; many seasons and means of conversion lost or taken from him by the sin or folly of others; and the root became ineradicable, and conscience at last was silent. Then came the end. *Recordare Jesu pie, quod sum causa tuae viae, ne me perdas ilia die.*

2. Next, there is the death of a careless priest. He has had only one enemy, but the worst enemy of all, treacherous, ubiquitous, and ever about him — that is, himself; an easy, yielding, indolent will. He has made no enemies, for he has not been in earnest enough about anything to

offend anybody. All men speak well of him. The character of priesthood has in him no visible and unmistakable outline. He is a welcome visitor, a pleasant companion, a ready and amusing guest, read up in the newspapers, and full of the events of the day. He is what is called a general favourite, hurting nobody but himself, and that so secretly that only God, his angel guardian, his confessor, and perhaps some unknown and watchful friend can see it. He does not see, or hardly sees it himself. His preparation for Mass is never altogether omitted, but it is short and hurried: his Mass is rapid — about twenty minutes — and mechanical: his thanksgiving is short and soon over: his office is said unpunctually, hurriedly, and with little attention spiritual or intellectual. Midnight overtakes him before he has said Prime, and he says the Rosary as a missionary privilege, without the exempting labour of a missionary priest. And yet he will go to his sick calls; sometimes, indeed, they are neglected, and sometimes he goes too late. When by the bedside of the dying, he is roused to a consciousness that he is in his place as a priest, but out of his place as a man. He gives the Sacraments and says the prayers in the Ritual. Then comes a silence. He has nothing to say. The habit of his life and the current of his thoughts are so remote from death and eternity that he has little to say. The dying soul is disappointed, and the friends standing by are saddened and vexed. When death overtakes such a priest it finds him little prepared. Perhaps he has not had forethought enough to send for some brother priest, and therefore, time being short, the last Sacraments come too late. How shall such a priest be saved from the sentence: "My people have been silent," in prayer and praise, "because they had no knowledge," through the neglect of their pastor: "because thou hast rejected knowledge, I will reject thee, that thou shalt not do the office of priesthood to Me."?[308]

3. Then comes the death of a lax priest. Laxity differs from carelessness in this. A careless priest may set up in his mind a high standard, and may draw strict theories of duty. But through carelessness he does not act up to them. A lax priest lowers his standard and minimises his obligations. He defends all opinions that favour human liberty, and looks upon strictness as rigour and Jansenism. He dwells largely on the first half of S. Paul's words. *Omnia mihi licent*, and passes dry-shod over the last, "*sed omnia non aedificant.*" He maintains that there are only two states, the one of liberty and the other of three vows: that the state of liberty is for those who do not aspire to be perfect, and the state of vows for those who are aiming at perfection. He directs those who are under his guidance to avoid two things, sin and strictness: to avoid sin, of course; but to avoid strictness, as leading to scruples and as hindering liberty. Such priests excuse in themselves many things by the plea, "I am not a religious" and "I am only a secular priest." They are never at a loss for probable doctors and various opinions. They have *communis opinio, et sine periculo tenenda*, for all they wish. It will never be known till the secret of all hearts shall be revealed what havoc such men make in the spiritual life of those who are guided or influenced by them. The direct effect of such laxity is to discourage aspiration for perfection among the faithful whose lot is cast in the world. And yet all

---

[308] Osee iv. 6.

Christians are called to be perfect, in whatsoever state of life. They would, indeed, try to keep people out of sin, but leave them upon the low level of a life, harmless, but without "hunger or thirst for justice." Such a life, if out of sin, is often in the occasions of sin. Liberty goes into the world and into all its laxities so long as sin is not manifest. But the world is covered with a network of occasions, as the veil of covering which is spread over all nations. Where one escapes a score are taken in the meshes. Now a priest who so instructs other souls assuredly first uses himself the liberty he gives so freely. And there can be no doubt that as a strict priest has both peace and sweetness in the restriction of his liberty, a lax priest has little of either in the freedom he allows himself. Theology cannot hold out for ever against conscience: sooner or later he begins to suspect and to see that he has forfeited fervour and aspiration and the "multitude of sweetness" which God has hid for those who fear Him. He has made his priesthood a yoke instead of a law of liberty. When such a priest comes to die, he often has little brightness, or joy, or confidence. He has not dealt generously with his Master, and in his last need he finds too late that they who have most denied themselves for His sake are most like Him; and that they are most free who have offered up their liberty by daily sacrifices of lawful things. A sad retrospect when life is ending: *Erubescet aliquando reus videri qui semper fuerat judex*.

4. After the lax priest comes the worldly priest, the true secular in name and spirit. He finds at last that he has served the wrong master, that in trying to serve two masters he has earned "wages to

put it into a bag with holes."[309] The world is passing from him, leaving him empty-handed, and in the eternal world which is opening he has laid up little reward. I am not now speaking of the worldly priests of ages past, but of worldliness as it may infect us still in the nineteenth century. The ambitious rivalries and contentions of other days, when priests were courtiers, and the Church was rich and in honour, are indeed passed away. But the world has other snares for priests — popularity, flattery, pleasure, corrupt and ruin many. They make many a priest to be fond of society, of ease, of dissipation, of comfort, of indulgence in food, in conversation, in refined pleasures of literature and music, and the arts and fashions of luxury. The effect of all this is to make the life of a presbytery dull and monotonous, the long hours of the confessional irksome, the visiting of the sick and the poor repulsive, the study of sacred books tasteless, the society of priests tame and uninteresting. The world has stolen away the heart of such a priest. It is no longer in his silent room, nor in the fellowship of his brethren, nor in the sanctuary, nor in his priesthood. It is somewhere abroad, in some house, or in some friendship, or in some intimacy. And when such a priest comes to die he cannot choose but cast up his reckoning, and make a *horarium* of his life. How many hours have I spent at the altar, and how many in the world? how many in the homes of the poor, and how many in the homes of the rich? how many in teaching little children, or consoling the afflicted, or in giving help to the dying? and how many in conversation over dinner-tables or in drawing-rooms? How many hours have I wasted in

---

[309] Aggeus i. 6.

wandering to and fro from house to horse, where I never heard and never uttered the name of God? and how much time have I spent in preaching His Word, the chief end of my priesthood? How many hours have I given to some particular friendship, and how many to prayer, speaking with God? Cast up these hours, turn them into days and years, and what a reckoning will stand before us. But it is already cast up in the book of God's remembrance. If the worldly priest had given the energy and diligence which he wasted on the world to the work of his own perfection, he might have been a Saint.[310]

5. Lastly — for we must end — comes the death of a fervent priest. The world never knew him, or passed him over as a dim light outshone by the priests who court it. But in the sight of God what a contrast. Ever since his ordination, or earlier, ever since his second conversion to God, he has examined his conscience day by day, and made up his account year by year; he has never failed in his confession week by week, or in his Mass morning by morning, or in his office punctually and in due season. He has lived as if by the side of his Divine Master, and, beginning and ending the day with Him, he has ordered all the hours and works of the day for His service. He has lived among his people, and their feet have worn the threshold of his door. His day comes at last, and a great sorrow is upon all homes when it is heard that the father of the flock is dying, and the last Sacraments have

---

[310] "Ecce mundus sacerdotibus plenus est, sed tamen in messe Dei rarus valde invenitur operator: quia officium quidam sacerdotale suscipimus, sed opus officii non implemus." — S. Greg. Hom. xvii. in Evangelia

been given to him. And yet in that dying-room what peace and calm. He has long cast up his reckoning for himself and for his flock. He has long talked familiarly of death, as of a friend who is soon coming. He fears it, as an awful transit from this dim world to the great white Throne, and as a sinner, an unprofitable servant, and a creature of the dust, he shrinks; for the Holy Ghost has taught him to know the sanctity of God and the sinfulness of sin. But it is a fear that casts out fear, for it is a pledge that the Holy Ghost, the Lord and Life-giver, is in the centre of his soul, casting light upon all that is to be confessed and sorrowed for, and absolving the contrite soul from all bonds of sin and death. None die so happily as priests surrounded by their flocks. As they have laboured, so are they loved; as they are loved, so are they sustained by the prayers of all whom they have brought to God. Wonderful bond of charity; closer and more vital than kindred, which shall be transfigured in the world of light, and unite pastor and flock to all eternity, when the flock shall all be told and the number be fulfilled, and the shepherds shall gather round the Great Shepherd of the sheep in the fold upon the everlasting hills.

If such be the death of a fervent priest it may be sudden: it cannot be unprepared. His whole life is a preparation for death. S. Charles as he departed said, *Ecce venio*, but his whole life was a continual approach to God. S. Vincent of Paul said, *Ipse perficiet*, as God was finishing His work in him. S. Hilarion said: "I have served a good Master for these seventy years; why should I be afraid to go and see Him?" S. Bede passed away on the eve of the Ascension, saying the antiphon, *O Rex gloriae,*

Domine virtutum; and S. Andrew Avellino died at, the foot of the altar, saying, *Introibo ad altare Dei*. A deacon in Africa, in the days of persecution, was singing the Easter Alleluias in the Ambo, when an arrow pierced his heart and he ended his Alleluias before the Throne. Some have fallen as they preached the Word of God. Happy, too, were they. Such a death, though sudden, has no fear, but great benediction. It is well to bear this ever in mind, leaving the time and the way of our end in the hands of our good Master. It would make us more fervent if, when we go to the altar, we were to say: "This may be my last Mass;" or in our confession, "This may be my last absolution;" or in preaching, "This may be the last time I shall speak for God;" or "This may be my last sick call — the next may be a call to me." How many companions of my childhood, boyhood, and manhood are dead. How many ordained with me or after me are gone before me. *Venire differt ut minus inveniat quod condemnet.* Wash me, Lord, in Thy most Precious Blood; and then, "Come, Lord Jesus."[311]

THE END.

---

[311] Apoc. xxii. 20.

Made in the USA
Monee, IL
28 June 2024